THE PRAYERS THAT HE PRAYED FOR ME

Sherry E. (Jones) Bobbitt

THE PRAYERS THAT HE PRAYED FOR ME

Edited and published by:
WOG Publishing
229 Took Drive
Antioch, TN 37013

Front Cover Design: Mario Johnson

Back Cover Photo: Sherry E. (Jones) Bobbitt

Scripture quotations marked KJV are from the King James Version.

ISBN: 978-1-955562-02-7

Printed in the U.S.A. by 48 Hour Books
www.48HrBooks.com

ACKNOWLEDGEMENTS

Special thanks, with love, to some very important people. First, I truly THANK God for the gift of writing and choosing a time such as this to do so.

Much love has come from writing this book. The strength that it took is more than I can express. There were so many memories, tears, heartache and meltdowns.

Ms. Paulette Kirkwood, a beloved teacher who loved and taught many at Northwest High School in St. Louis, Missouri. This wonderful teacher saw something in me that I couldn't see in myself and wasn't trying to see. I just wanted to get through the assignments and get an A, but she pulled me aside from time to time and let me have it. Always firm with me, so firm that there were times that I felt like she didn't like me, and I couldn't understand why. As I got older and began to utilize my gift, after winning my very first 1st place trophy, her words whispered to me, and I realized that it was never about not liking me. She was loving, nurturing, molding and shaping me. I was so blessed to tell her "Thank you" at a Northwest Alumni Christmas party. I also told her about my first book of many that I had to write.

Additionally, I told her that I cannot do so without mentioning her contribution to my life. Teachers are very special people…some more exceptional than others. Ms. Kirkwood is one. I hope that I have made you very proud of me.

My parents would tell anybody that I didn't get this from them. They just considered me going through a lot of notebook paper back in the day until they both had the opportunity to read and hear me recite my work. They were both proud of me, especially my mom. She nearly caused me to stop writing not realizing that it was a gift. I am glad to know they are proud of me. I wish they were here for this season in my life. Rest well dear parents. Forever your #1 child. I truly miss Tyrone Jones and Clarice Ann (Ms. Classy) Jones. I would be remiss not to acknowledge my loving stepmother, Henrietta Brown Jones. We never used the word "step" as our relationship was deeper than that. At this writing, I am happy to say that I am blessed to still have her 100-year-old mother, Majorie Tate, with us. Growing up, my paternal grandparents and great grandparents (Elizabeth Jones Brown, Mildred and Elnora Barnett, Hurlie and Louise Carnes) deposited many nuggets of wisdom which I still pull from.

My siblings Ronald Tyrone Jones, Keisha Lynn Jones, Anthony Brown, Charlene Brown, Reginald Brown and Kevin Brown for believing in me and always saying how gifted their Tutter is. Although Reginald and Kevin are deceased, their love and support for the 'Glitter Queen' still remains in my heart and means so much to me. Each of my siblings have always supported my being different—a one of a kind—and will tell anybody, that's my big sister just doing what she does.

My Godfather, Mr. William (Bill) Holt, bka Uncle Bill. He has been there for me since day one. I can't remember many important things in my life when Uncle Bill wasn't there to celebrate my accomplishments. A special thank you to Mr. Mike Henry and his parents, Mr. Roland and Ms. Berta Henry.

My loving aunts and uncles have been so supportive, being listening ears for me to talk to in the places of my parents. My cousins all celebrate their big cousin.

TABLE OF CONTENTS

REFLECTIONS

The twain flesh becomes one in God. One plus one equals two. This book is an excellent manifestation of what constitutes a marriage relationship that is God centered.

What you are about to read is not about human perfection, but human imperfection made right by the Creator who is perfect. This is a powerful example of what can be achieved when prayer is included in a marriage, from a rough undone state to Godly romantic bliss.

I have had many conversations with Sherry and James about this book which was their dream. Now it has become a reality. James' prayers have been answered.

The care given to James by Sherry could only have come through Agape love which is sincere love that was reciprocated. They have shared with us many lessons to be learned in marriage relationships while on this spiritual journey.

Johnny Ray Thomas
Jackson, TN

*****

The prayers that are recorded in this book reflect a husband's deep love and commitment to his wife "Sugar Britches", as he affectionately called her. James, her husband, was not perfect (as none of us are), yet he prayed perseveringly for her and for their marriage. He held both of them in the highest esteem and desired God's very best for them and their lives together.

The prayers he prayed were birthed out of a humble and sincere heart, a heart that always desired to encourage and propel Sherry (Sugar Britches) in her gift of writing. His prayers are reminiscent of the passage in Hebrews 7:25 about our beloved bridegroom Jesus, who "...always lives to make intercession for us."

As you read this book, may God draw you closer to Himself and give you the courage to step into your gifting. I pray that He will be glorified in the work that He has called you to do.

Monica Kennedy, Retired
Smyrna, TN

*****

I have known James and Sherry Bobbitt for over 20 years and what a blessing they both have been. Being an eyewitness to their unique and intimate relationship allowed my husband and me to be somewhat of a beneficiary. There was never a question in my mind as to whether or not Sherry would write, but just a matter of when. When the Lord blessed James and Sherry to experience a union built on a praying personality, His divine intent is that other lives and relationships would be impacted. I am grateful that God connected our paths so many years ago. Blessings to you James and Sherry Bobbitt!

Pastor Marilyn McClain
Nashville, TN

*****

At the time of this book being written, the writer is in the process of healing from many storms from early childhood until the present. This is not fiction, but real-life experiences and it, hopefully, will help the reader think before making these same decisions. From losing an only child, emergency surgery, parental abuse, sibling abuse and friend betrayal, the writer has been a victim of many storms. The storms are finally calming, and she is beginning to spread her wings. She has not let family drama, workplace stress, nor personal issues deter her from spreading her wings and soaring like an eagle above the storms that she has endured. Farewell to the storm! Hello to the positive side of life!

Wilmatine H. Elam, Retired Professor
Nashville, TN

*****

One of the most important parts of a marriage relationship is communication. What is needed for that communication to be intact and healthy is "prayer" to our Heavenly Father; really keeping Him in the middle of every situation.

What God has allowed my sista and friend Sherry Jones Bobbitt to pen through the pages of her and my beloved brother James Bobbitt's life is awesome. "The Prayers That He Prayed For Me" has so many nuggets, layers and levels to learn from…the good, the bad and the ugly. All of it was/is a teachable moment.

I know with all of Sherry's transparency and descriptions, and I would go as far to say prescriptions for a healthy relationship, James's prayers for his wife will help to heal many relationships and to see themselves on the other side of their situation. It will spark, inspire and give many relationships a way out of some of the pitfalls they may be going through or may go through in their life. (In Jesus Name)!

Sherry Goodlow Allen, Airline Attendant
Jennnings, LA

*****

After having to stop and take tissue breaks because of memories relived and my heart's reaction to beautiful testimonies that only the heart can understand, my Tutta (Sherry), let me say to you how proud as a peacock I am of you and my brother James Lynn Bobbitt. You remind me of a butterfly. How we delight in its beauty and colors, but as we delight in it, we seldom think about what it took for that beauty to become something we could enjoy.

All the changes it has gone through to get that beauty and achieve and delight in that beauty. Through your journey and your battles like the butterfly you have come forth with strength, courage, change, transformation and comfort. And now you are flying beyond your cocoon of hurt, rejection, lies, discouragement, embarrassment, pain, and hopelessness by the grace of God because of the prayers he (James) prayed for you. Butterflies show us how we can go within ourselves to dissolve the old and change, rebuild, and evolve ourselves. You, my Tutta (Sherry), have spread your beautiful wings. Now fly beautiful butterfly!!!!

Your Tutta
Lady/Minister Freda Cousin
Nashville, TN

*****

It is rare that I have the opportunity to read a book. A book about a real person pouring out her compassionate and raw heart about two of many things I value in life: Prayer and Covenant. Sherry has a bold, comical and innocent way of telling about treasured, sweet and challenging moments in time of her life with her husband. There is a richness in her honesty that encourages you to keep turning the page for the next laugh, the next "Oh No!", the next tear, and the next...

Yes, you never know what will come next as you read every word that tumbled from her heart and glided on every page. Couples? Singles? Or just those who love to cuddle up to a good book that undoubtedly carries you through time and stirs your heart to wonder about love and loss.

Grab your favorite hot cup of yummy. Slip into your coziest comforts. Light a tropical candle next to a warm lamp and sit in your big easy chair, turn the pages and allow your imagination to drift to the world of covenant love with Sherry Jones Bobbitt. (Don't forget your box of tissues.)

Crystal Joy, M.Ed.
Clarksville, TN
Dept. Head of Living Parables Drama Ministry
Host of WQQK - Joy in the Morning Show

*****

What can we say, the raw true emotions, honesty and transparency displayed in the book is mind blowing. We laughed, cried, we learned so much. Thank you so much for sharing your story with us and teaching that in marriage we will struggle but CHRIST must be the center and truly love conquers it all. This book shows us that the only third person's voice we should be listening to is God. Keep your family, friends, and neighbors out of your business. Sherry, truly your gifting and anointing in this book will transform, refresh, and bring revival to brokenness in marriages. Keep walking in faith and putting words to paper. God bless you. God will use your story for His glory. We love you with the love of the Lord.

Dec. Curtis and Christine Coleman
aka Boaz and Tutta
Pittsburgh, PA

*****

The Prayers That He Prayed is a true masterpiece. In life, the most valuable items found gained their value from surviving the most horrific moments. The marriage relationship is such an item. Once you open up this book, you find yourself gauging and identifying areas within your marriage and/or relationship that have denied God's invitation and personal attention. I see value in prayer in marriage clearer now. Thank you, Sherry, for revealing strategy and war tactics that are necessary for restoring the breach.

This is a story that has been written in such a way that opens up one's understanding of what God intended marriage to be.

Pastor Dannetta Moore
Benton Harbor, MI
*****

Rarely do I read a book that keeps my attention to continue turning the pages because of its content. I found this book to be an easy read filled with life experiences between two people who did what they deemed best to keep their marriage filled with life and love. The author wrote in such a pellucid manner rending a pictorial view into the life that she shared with her beloved husband James. It takes much courage to put pen to paper and expose your life to be used as a tool for others to learn. This is truly a book that should be read.

Mike Henry
Collinsville, IL

*****

The first time James prayed for Sherry brought me to an old school song from Percy Sledge *When a Man Loves a Woman*. Percy speaks of him not being able to keep his mind on anything else and how he would trade the world, appreciating the good thing he found. He went on to speak about not being able to see any bad in her and how she could do no wrong, and about his willingness to turn his back on others to make sure she was secure. Additionally, he spoke of spending his last dime, giving up his comforts, even sleeping out in the rain, never allowing another woman to receive a hug or his attention; his loving eyes were only for her. This book is a true love story. It has its share of ups and downs, and some unbelievable moments, but what counted the most is that they did it together. Sherry and James are an inspiration to all those who are desiring and trying to define what true love is. As a newlywed, I pray that my husband and I only have eyes for one another as shown by James and Sherry and that we endure warfare together and, most importantly, keep GOD first. Bless you Sherry for allowing me this opportunity to be a part of such a vulnerable yet beautiful part of your life. You are such a Godsend and ray of sunshine. May God continue to bless you and keep you.

Love, Pastor Amanda Key
Nashville, TN

*****

From a man's perspective…this book provides a perspective that most of us never consider. The author proves to us that when a husband stands as the Priest in his home, there are women/wives that long for men to take our proper stance in the home/ relationship. When we do, the relationship is valued on a greater level.

Pastor Mario A. Johnson
Clarksville, TN

*****

The elements of love are so essential. When there is love, there is life. This is absolutely necessary in order for oneness to be in a relationship. Love will lead you to a life that will have you to embrace each other in multiple ways. Love promotes commitment in prayer, faithfulness, and unity.

Prayer is open communication with each other and God. It does not matter what condition you're in, there is always room for prayer and love. Love can sometimes place you out of your comfort zone and open you up to the needs of each other, rather than your own desires. When we seek God, he will lead us into the new environments of selfless love. You will find many examples of selfless love in the ups and downs of marriage in the lives of the Bobbitts.

This book is intended to encourage, promote, and provide examples of transparency, consistency, and selflessness. You will find this book as an encouragement to truly understand that prayer and love is what creates the foundation for a Godly marriage!

Bishop-Elect Dr. Monterey D. Lee, Sr.
Celebration Christian Center, Inc.
Murfreesboro, TN

*****

Growing up in Walnut Park, St. Louis wasn't always easy, but the love you felt was special. Having a close relationship with the author since childhood makes this book very easy to understand the love, compassion, communication, and prayer they had for themselves and each other. Their journey in their individual lives makes you feel like the saying "made for each other" is truly about them. James was a loving husband that continued to learn the power of prayer in all the areas mentioned throughout the book. Your attention and focus go from they are doing it to asking yourself how can I also learn from their experiences of intentional love of each other, cherish each other and keeping God involved? You will be on a great ride while looking into the lives of a very loving, committed husband and wife expressing and showing each other that no matter what happens, we can commit to make sure we are "until death do us part." My neighbor and friend of forty-five years will not disappoint you while experiencing a journey full of love, compassion, hurt, understanding, and communicating to make sure they both operate in God's will.

Troy Rhodes
St. Louis, MO
*****

Every marriage has its challenges aka Hurricane Season. Sherry's openness to share hers speaks to the strength we all have if willing to survive the storms of embarrassment, shame, homelessness, spiritual confusion, the betrayal of family and friends and the list goes on. But true love lasts forever – even to the grave.

This book caused me to appreciate my husband of 40+ years even more. This would be a good book to use in a marriage ministry. Be blessed aka Sugar Britches.

Judy Johnson, Senior Pastor of Claiborne Family of Faith Worship
Center and WVOL 1470 AM Radio Talk Show Host
Nashville, TN

*****

My friendship with Sherry is traced back to our childhood at Walnut Park neighborhood. I am more of a big brother than a friend. This story is a testament to the power of prayer and the resilience of the human spirit. In all the storms she faced, she chose love. We meet a woman whom, in the face of challenges, turned to prayer as a source of hope and guidance. The pain and hurt caused by mistrust almost broke their marriage, but they both fought hard to overcome it.

Her experience taught me the need to be intentional in marriage and to choose personalized prayer for those we love. Through James's heartfelt prayers, she discovered a deeper connection with herself, her partner, and with God. I did not have the privilege of interacting with James, but the book has demonstrated the beauty of what love can do in marriage. This story is a powerful reminder that no matter how difficult the situation may seem, there is always hope. With faith, perseverance, and the courage to face our challenges head on, we can overcome even the toughest of obstacles. That is, if we give our very best into loving those close to us, we will walk far and discover a beauty for the people around us. So, whether you are currently facing challenges in your own marriage, or simply looking for inspiration and guidance on your journey, this book is sure to leave a lasting impression. It is a story of love, forgiveness, and redemption, and a testament to the power of prayer to transform our lives. This book is a testament to the power of love and faith in a marriage. It shows how even in the face of adversity, we can still hold on to our beliefs and fight for what is right. The author's journey is one that will inspire and encourage anyone who has ever experienced the pain of mistrust in a relationship.

I reread Sherry's piece again and again trying to understand the best approach of sustaining a marriage in the brink of collapse. First of all, it was musical. It had echoes of Galway Kinnell, "If one day it happens you find yourself with someone you love in a café at one end of the Pont Mirabeau, at the zinc bar where white wine stands in upward opening glasses (taken from Astonishments by Kinnell). It also had a taste of something else. Something from far land. Before zinc bars. Something of art, where we are able to develop a passion of something that we want to devour so much.

This story has introduced me to this couple. I experienced honesty, a truth in the writing that stopped me in my tracks. I learned that no matter how difficult the journey, there is always hope for a better tomorrow. You will learn that marriages do not have to break; that we do not have to disconnect from our loved ones, just the way Sherry tried to do. When we are intentional about our marriages, we will get the divine guidance to hold on. I encourage you to read this book with an open heart and mind. Let the author's story inspire you to fight for your own relationships and to always hold on to hope, even in the darkest of times. See how love sounds. See how brave it is to reveal your love like this. See how love in difficult situations feels. See what it is to live and love, to trust that person with whom you have experienced both love and pain, to influence the lives of others after the marriage has been done away with because of death. Today we are bombarded with distractions at every turn, asynchronous communication, mobile phones, TVs, and ephemera. Stop and experience this dialogue with my little sister, Sherry. Listen to her. In the silences between her words, listen to what she is not saying. Therein lies her message. I experienced it; I hope you will, too. It is an invaluable gift.

Henry Williams
Retired Fire Chief and City Manager of Berkeley in St. Louis County MO

FROM THE AUTHOR

This book is undoubtedly assigned to me by God. Additionally, my husband, James, wanted me to write this book after his passing. He told me that I would understand why if I respected his wishes as to when to write it. I have three other books forthcoming, but this is the one that James wanted written first. Our prayer is that this book reminds some and to introduce other ***married*** couples to just how crucial it is to have a **healthy** prayer life together in the marriage relationship.

It is often said: There Is Power in Prayer! The POWER - God's POWER through prayer together puts power in your marriage relationship. Two people coming together on one accord lovingly touching for the purpose of Oneness. The Oneness in their marriage relationship ensures a marriage bond so tightly knitted together with only a decision from God to separate the two from remaining as one. We considered prayer long before marriage as the needed *fertilizer* to allow our marriage roots to become so lovingly strong that it would withstand any storm that we encountered and for us it did just that.

I will be sharing the prayers that James prayed for me, along with the story that took place leading to the prayers. We believed that God could fix any problem we faced. A healthy prayer life together, and inviting God in the WHOLE marriage which includes the bedroom. Yes, I said ***THE BEDROOM***! Why? Why not? If you know me, I'm going to keep it 1000! I am more transparent than most. The call on my life is not yours; therefore, I must move in the direction that God leads me.

Here are some reasons why ***THE BEDROOM***. Some issues with a marriage relationship start in the bedroom. Everyone knows that this is true, but who really talks about it? We did...Mr. and Mrs. James Lynn Bobbitt. The first time that James and I heard the phrase a "sexless marriage" we couldn't believe that there was such a thing. To grow apart from each other sexually while married is truly a reason to pray. It was a reason for us to pray because we didn't want that for us. The marriage relationship has bedroom issues. For some married couples a lack of sexual contact and lovemaking becomes a big issue. After a while, a lack of intimacy becomes a huge problem. The bedroom is a place where many important conversations take place. The bedroom is:

* the main area of the home where sex, intimacy and heated romantic moments occur.
* a place for play, sharing, watching tv, reading together, snuggling and sleeping together.
* the place where you take care of each other when illnesses come.
* a place where married couples are extremely transparent.
* a place where disagreements happen.
* a place just to lay quiet with each other.
* a place to pray together and study God's word.

What a very special place the bedroom is in the lives of a married couple!

PREFACE

A Perfect Combination for your Marriage Relationship
God and a Prayer Life Together

Of course, you should have your own personal prayer time but what a difference it makes when you develop one together. This book has not been written for you and your spouse to pray exactly like James and I did but to encourage the two of you to develop and enjoy your own healthy prayer life together, having that very special time with God and each other.

A healthy prayer life together won't prevent stormy seasons from happening, but it will certainly help both to go through them with an even flow for a good and positive outcome. I can't express enough the magnitude of the power in prayer.

Before I started writing this book, I was taken aback by the number of believers who don't have a healthy prayer life together, especially among Church leadership. I will probably say this throughout this book that this is shocking to me. I actually thought that I could get some insight on other healthy prayer lives together among church leadership and their spouses.

Some may agree, some may disagree, but I believe this book will show the importance of a healthy prayer life among leadership. I wonder how much leadership properly and effectively counsels other marriages when their marriage doesn't have a prayer life. Just my thoughts on the situation, yet so much is preached and taught about a life without prayer.

Prayer aids in:

* being able to agree to disagree without falling out with each other which can lead to division.
* always respecting each other even during times of being upset.
* helps to move forward without harboring ill feelings.
* not magnifying situations.
* remembering that you are a team.

* not deeming it always necessary who is/was right or wrong.
* being willing to forgive each other's mistakes.
* remembering the vows that you pledged to each other.
* not using issues from the past to undermine each other.
* keeping out negative interference and unwise advice/counsel, but instead holding on tight to each other during stormy seasons and trying times as God holds the both of you together.

Wrapped Up in His Divine Love and Comfort!

I can imagine some readers will think where was God when your hurricane season occurred? Well, my answer to that is, "Has God answered every prayer that you have prayed?" I already know the answer. There are so many things in life that I prayed for like my babies. I wanted children, but that never happened, and I dealt with it like other unexplainable things that happen in life.

I am writing this book with many, many, many tears, sweet precious memories, bad memories, pain, anger, loneliness, sadness, plenty of laughs, smiles, joy and missing my husband with every stroke of my pen. I can truly say it was pain that brought me here, but my deep passion for love and marriage gives me the strength that I need in this new season, new life without James. This is a season that I did not ask for or want. Transitioning from Mrs. to Ms. Bobbitt has been a challenge for me, especially when I absolutely adored being Mrs. James Lynn Bobbitt. This was one of the things that I promised him. His belief in me has also brought me to this place in time...one from which I am still learning while on this journey without him.

God has blessed me with the gift of writing, and I must utilize my gift during this unexpected journey in my life. I truly miss the prayer life that I had with my husband, him anointing me with oil, laying hands on me and praying. Sometimes, I find it very hard to pray since he's been gone. Some may say that my roots in God weren't very strong to begin with, my faith had to be weak. Whatever your take is on this, is just your take on it.

Until you have the experience of losing a loving spouse, you can't possibly know and it's ok. I don't wish this experience on anyone, but I have had people from many different levels of leadership to change their tune with my views now that they have lost their spouse.

I truly get that when life without James gets my emotions all over the place (as many have stressed to me) that God can hold me and comfort me in the midnight hours. I know this but I have to keep it real. I really miss my husband rocking me in the midnight hours, two totally different needs. That comes with time to get used to. Those feelings didn't leave just because James had to leave me, not at all.

No matter where James and I prayed, after every AMEN we sealed it with a kiss, even over the phone. If the setting that we were in did not allow us to stand side by side holding hands while prayer was being rendered, we blew a kiss to each other. We would always extend our pinky fingers out in a curled position when we could be side by side, always on the marriage hand, something that he started, and I thought was so cute.

Our prayer life together meant so much to us. We knew that we needed God to be with us as a married couple. He would often say "I know that we need this Sugar Britches because the devil does not want me to be the Godly man that God has called me to be, and you are the chosen woman just for me. If we don't pray, we won't last and too many people will rejoice."

The prayer life that we had together means so much more to me now because sharing our story, my pain, I am finding out that so many married couples don't have a prayer life together. We actually thought that married couples always prayed together. It was very shocking the few times when we found out differently. Some married couples would express that only one of them went to church or neither went to church. James would say "What does that have to do with you praying together?" Then we would share how our prayer life together began. I would truly catch them by surprise, but it was us simply keeping it real. The bigger shock was the lack of a prayer life together among pastors, ministers and deacons.

We didn't get this from within the church walls or wise counsel from someone who sat us down and poured into us. It came through James praying alone, seeking God concerning me to become his wife. With that, I choose to believe that God spoke to James' heart to speak to my heart for our heart (as one heart). We wanted to keep the heart of oneness that developed in our boyfriend/girlfriend relationship before marriage.

I firmly believe that keeping the boyfriend and girlfriend in our marriage relationship was truly a blessing for us. Why? James didn't fall in love with me as his wife, he first fell in love with me as his girlfriend and asked his girlfriend to become his wife. Accordingly, I had to make sure that he had more than enough reasons to fall in love with his wife too. Just my take on it. You, the reader, may think differently but this is OUR story and what worked for us.

Smiling with tears in my eyes as I write this because prayer was so very important to James and I, for those who knew him, knew the value he placed on it. He would say:

- Prayer keeps the oneness in our marriage.
- Prayer keeps our love growing for each other every day.
- Baby, prayer keeps you understanding me when I don't understand myself.
- Prayer keeps you loving me regardless of my many flaws and every imperfect fiber in me.
- Prayer has allowed you to feel my heart when I am upset, even when we are miles apart. I can count on a call from you to see what is going on.
- Prayer has given you so much patience. Most women would have walked away from me and never looked back.
- Prayer has blessed you with a special gift to keep loving me in my deepest struggles with myself. You have always spoken life into me even when I was choosing a road of darkness.
- Sherry, you always thank God that I am a praying man, but you don't realize that I could not be that man if you were not a

strong praying woman. And Sugar Britches, that is so very special and precious to me.

Believe it or not, but it was James who chose our wedding theme – "We are One". Oneness meant a lot to him. He also felt that prayer was his personal reassurance that God would do everything that was impossible for him to do in our marriage and for me. His key scripture for our marriage was Proverbs 18:22 (KJV) "Whoso findeth a wife findeth a good thing, and obtaineth favour of the Lord." A few months before he transitioned from this life, he began to quote Proverbs 18:22 from The Message Bible which says, "Find a good spouse, you find a good life and even more the favor of God!" A few weeks before he left me, he would say it with tears rolling down his cheeks, smiling and then say, "Sugar Britches thank you for a good life, one that you didn't have to share with me because I didn't always do right." The day before he transitioned, he told his mother what that scripture meant to him and that he had the favor of God through me. It was just how he felt.

One of the reasons that I did not reach the deadline that I set for myself with this writing is all of the emotions and things that I couldn't see. So many things that I didn't understand, I understand now as I am writing this book. I didn't understand that it was some of our last conversations, smiles, tears and prayers together. Why? Because I was truly believing God for a miracle. I was holding fast to my faith. I saw, in my heart, my husband standing in Olivet Missionary Baptist Church with that "But God" testimony! One of those "Don't Count Me Out" testimonies that people get to give. He was thanking me and saying "it's my time" but I didn't hear that because of what I was believing God for! I just assumed that he was preparing himself for months and months later.

Sometimes I feel that maybe, just maybe it wasn't meant for me to know that he was getting ready to rest but it still brings me to tears. People have often said to me that I shouldn't have wanted him to suffer. I never wanted him to suffer. I was looking for a miracle and expecting the impossible. People can certainly say some hurtful things…meaning well, at least I hope they meant well.

My prayer is that this book (our story) will inspire married couples as well as couples who are engaged to become married and married couples who may be considering divorce. I pray you are enriched by the power of prayer and giving God the room and time to bless your marriage relationship. At the end of each chapter are our songs that I encourage the reader to listen to. There are times in life when a song can convey what is in your heart better than words.

James believed in my gift to write and was my biggest cheerleader. He wanted me to write this story. I always thought that my journey for our story would begin at 75 years of age, never did I think that I would be at 53.

Please pray before and after reading "The Prayers That He Prayed for Me" and the reasons for each prayer in this book. Please allow God, through prayer, to elevate your marriage relationship to reach levels of love and joy that you've never dreamed of before. Allow God to remove any past hurts and residue from stormy seasons and to cleanse your heart from death spoken words.

Seize the golden opportunity to greet each given day together as it yields another chance to make new memories and love each other more than you did the day before! We only have our right now. We can make plans for so many tomorrows as married couples, but they aren't promised to us. I know this all too well now.

Allow me to share some "intentionals" with you. The word intentionally means deliberately, on purpose. So...

- Intentionally Love Each Other
- Intentionally Choose to Be in Love With Each Other
- Intentionally Cherish Each Other
- Intentionally Respect Each Other
- Intentionally Adore Each Other
- Intentionally Pray with and for Each Other
- Intentionally Forgive Each Other
- Intentionally Hug and Kiss Each Other Daily
- Intentionally Agree to Disagree With Each Other
- Intentionally Smile At Each Other, Even in The Midst of a Storm
- Intentionally Date Each Other. Keep the boyfriend and girlfriend in the marriage relationship. (After all the boyfriend asked the girlfriend to become his wife, so why get rid of them?)
- Intentionally Enjoy Each Other
- Intentionally Stay in Love With Each Other, Doing Things to Keep the Fire Burning
- Intentionally Only Have Eyes For Each Other
- Intentionally Have Many, Many "Just Because" Moments {not doing special things only on special days}
- INTENTIONALLY!!! INTENTIONALLY!!! INTENTIONALLY!!! NEVER LEAVE GOD OUT OF YOUR MARRIAGE RELATIONSHIP!

~POEM~

Intentionally love like there is no tomorrow promised for you.
Precious moments spent together saturating each other like the midst of the early morning dew.

Intentionally keep the fire burning as if your love lives on a snowcapped mountain.
Allow the freshness of love at its finest to continue flowing like the beauty of a Paris fountain.

Intentionally refuse to allow words to harm and hurt your marriage.
Agree to disagree climbing together into your love carriage.

Intentionally pray together every day,
Giving God THE GLORY for making days blue when the enemy wants them gray.

Intentionally send each other off with sweet sentiments from the heart with a pleasant sound from your voice.
Leaving a sweet aroma that lingers on with other choice.

Intentionally embrace the just because moments that means more than you just care, Overwhelming the chamber of the heart that intensely moves in a romantic flow of fresh air.

Intentionally hold each other as much as you can enjoying the tenderness of a loving touch, Without words spoken the heart hears, I love you so much.

Intentionally stay **in** love **with** love together allowing its beauty to engulf your marriage with an overflow of life.
Intentionally on every level experience the joys of being husband and wife!

Author: Sherry E. (Jones) Bobbitt
My Song Choices: *I Believe You* by Dorothy Moore
The Right Kinda Lover by Patti LaBelle

CHAPTER 1: HIS FIRST PRAYER FOR ME

This is such a very special prayer for me because it caught me by surprise. I wasn't expecting this from him. My heart was truly on another level of love after this prayer – his first prayer for me.

Amazingly, the first time that James prayed for me was in a hotel room. Yes, a hotel room. He would always bless the food before eating but that was as far as it went when I was with him, and I really expected no more from him. I had never heard him pray like this. My mind was far from anything other than blessing the food. This certainly blew my mind. I must say it again, I was truly caught by surprise and amazed that he was so very serious and somewhat emotional too. We had only been dating for three weeks and he wanted to pray together and pray for me. I said "Ok." I really didn't know what to say or how to feel but still wondering out of all places, why in a hotel room?

The evening before, he picked me up like he always did. Strangely, he was very quiet and seemed to have something heavy on his mind. He was normally loud, talkative and jolly. Well, I just assumed that he had a hard day at work. I was extremely shy then, so I asked no questions, but I was very concerned. We went to dinner; he was still kind of quiet, but he just kept looking at me smiling and I was in a place wondering what is really going on but still never asked. After dinner we went to our spot (hotel room), we cuddled and kissed for a while, took a shower. I thought that we were going to get "busy", but he said he just wanted to hold me until we fall asleep. He said, "We have plenty of time and many years together to make love to each other.

I just want to hold you tonight; hold you as close to me as I can as if you were melting inside of me. I want our hearts beating at the same pace." After a while he said, "Mrs. Bobbitt I know that I told you when we first saw each other face to face that I loved you and on our first date I told you that you will be my wife – the only Mrs. James Lynn Bobbitt in the world and I need you to know that I just wasn't caught up in some moment. I meant every word and one day you will write about us." I said nothing, I just laid there in awe. We kissed and said good night to each other and just simply went to sleep.

It was the most peaceful sleep and the most enchanting morning to wake up and he was kissing me. Truly I was in my very own fairy tale, the only things that were missing was our enchanted castle and our golden carriage with four beautiful white horses. I was simply caught in my own little world. He got up and called his coworker, Marshall, to pick him up for work. He wanted me to take his car, go to my mom, take her to her doctor's appointment, do some shopping for us, do a few things for him and he would call me when he got to our spot. So, I did all that he asked of me. A little after 7:00 p.m. he called me to come to our spot. Feeling somewhat like a wife, I was on my way home and smiling all the way. Yet I couldn't help but wonder still what was on his mind, why the mood shifted. As soon as I turned onto the parking lot, there he was standing with that James Bobbitt smile, a smile that simply melted my heart. As I was parking, he said "Sugar Britches my girl, hey baby. I really missed you today. I'll get the bags." He opened the car door and kissed me like he hadn't seen me in weeks. We went into the room and there was a beautiful surprise waiting for me. The table was set for dinner with a bouquet of lilies. (I like lilies better than roses.) There was also a brown teddy bear with a gold chain necklace around its neck, a beautiful black teddy set, rose petals, scented candles and a bottle of wine. It was so romantically enchanting. He asked me what I thought. I said, "Oh my, how romantically enchanting with such sweet sentiments and thoughtfulness." He said, "Damn girl, I am going to have to get use to your way with words, but your eyes and smile says a lot more."

While sitting on the bed, he said, "I really need to talk to you, I mean seriously talk to you because I have never been more serious about somebody in my life." I said, "Okay." I got so nervous until I began to tremble. He said, "Sherry, it's nothing bad. I really believe that it will be the best things for us – me and you, just us." He took me by the hands and said, "Mrs. Bobbitt we need to start praying together. I must start praying for you, after all I will be the priest of our household, my love. You arc the queen of my heart. I can't say it enough. No matter what happens in life, you will be the only woman in this world who will be Mrs. James Lynn Bobbitt and I mean that." I said, "Ok." He smiled, got on his knees and asked me to join him. He prayed, he prayed for us and then he prayed for me. When he finished, we just cried, it was such an incredible feeling, one that neither of us had ever felt before. Something happened that evening…something that we couldn't put into words, but it happened. There was such a connection as if our hearts touched. We didn't eat, we just laid down and kept crying. I was laying up against his back. He put my hand on his heart and said, "I want you to always know when I need your hand right here, even when I don't realize that I need the comfort of your hand right here, promise me that you will always know." The last thing that I remember him saying was, "No other woman will reach my heart like this; I don't care what she has to offer me, this is your place and I hope that I am in the same place in your heart." I said for the first time "I Love You, Mr. James Lynn Bobbitt." He said, "Damn girl! I have waited to hear you say more than just ok". We laughed and went to sleep.

James gave me something on that night that I choose to refer to as ***Spiritual Intimacy***. I really don't know if there is such a thing, but it is how I choose to see it, express my feelings about what took place and I still do. I never felt that with no other man. James was my first, my only and that makes it more special than words can ever express. Nothing sexual about that special moment together, but truly a deep matter in our hearts. Over the years we talked about that moment and just always thanked God for a time such as it was.

He began his prayer that night thanking God for the day, the many blessings that HE bestowed upon us, he THANKED God for keeping him at home in Trenton because he was planning to move back to Nashville that weekend, then he saw me. He said, "LORD, I THANK YOU!" He asked for healing for both of our moms, (his mom was having severe back issues and my mom had a stroke which is the reason that I was in Trenton).

He asked that God would lead and guide him to become a Godly Man and husband that his grandmother told him that he could be, not to let his heart stray from God and me but if it did, let him please return to both of us.

Then James prayed for me! He said:

> LORD, please be with this precious diamond in the rough next to me - this diamond that the world has yet to see. Touch her heart and mind where she really understands just how much YOU love her and just how much that I love and need her too. This is my first time truly being in love. I thought in the past that I was, but I really know what it feels like because I feel her in my soul. Lord, YOU know that I pray for her more than I do for myself here lately. Give her the desires of her heart, open her mouth that she may speak what is in her beautiful heart, let her not be afraid for me to love her more than any man that she has known. There is so much inside of her that needs to come out to help others. She is a different kind of woman, protect her from everybody, including me, that may try to cause harm to her just to destroy her heart.
>
> Let her dreams come true. Show her how to love me, give me the love that I need, not just physical love but that special love that a man needs from his wife that keeps him covered in prayer…the kind of love that looks beyond his faults as you do. Let her know when I need her even when we are far apart. Let her love me through any storm that the devil may create to break us apart. Let her seek you for all things concerning me. Please don't take her childlike, little girlish ways of looking at life as always beautiful. Please help her to understand my ways, ways that I am looking for you to change. Give her patience as you are working within me LORD. Let her always have a forgiving heart. Let not any pain in her past keep her from

> being the woman you have called her to be. If, for some reason, that I get beside myself and try to stand in her way, give her the strength to stand up and obey you. She has such a beautiful inner makeup about her; let it be the light that guides me when I can't see or hear YOU, LORD. Every tear that she cries where I am at fault turn into joy. Let her love for me grow more and more each day we are together. Let her stand even when my family or her family comes up against her. Please don't ever let her leave me. Please, allow her and her love for me be for my forever as I stand by her side with my love to give in return. LORD, I ask this with my heart in my hand, my mind made up because she is the one that you sent, the one of my dreams, the one that I can count on through thick and thin, the one that will fill my heart and feel my heart. I know that she will. LORD, let her down in the DEEP TREASURES OF YOUR LOVE, JOY, PEACE and UNDERSTAND-ING so she may be that diamond in the rough that will shine differently, sparkle differently, whose words will only speak in a type of wisdom that may seem strange to many but comforting to most. Let her hands soothe the deep wounds in my heart just by a simple touch. Let her voice reach my soul and I never get to a point that I can't hear her. Bless her LORD only as you can, I ask this in the precious name of JESUS CHRIST. AMEN. AMEN. AMEN.

One may be thinking, how can she remember this prayer so well? It is very simple. James never stopped praying this prayer, he just added to it over the years.

Sealing that prayer with a kiss became a part of our prayer life together. If you really knew us as a couple, you knew that we kissed after prayer, and it didn't matter where we were. To this day I am speechless rendering words to express what this first prayer did to my spirit. There have been times that I referred to it as a beautiful prayer gift.

The next morning, we got up and drove way out in the country. He asked me to stay in the car and don't look back, just wait until he called me. Before he called me, I could hear *Summer Breeze* by The Isley Brothers playing. I got out of the car, turned around and, there he was on some quilts with nothing on but a smile. The bottle of Asti Spumante, fruit and cheese. Wow! One of my fantasies! So we just ??????????? okkkkkkkkkk!!!

This first chapter has been very emotional for me, my life, our story. As strange as some may find it, I wouldn't have it any other way – the way we were. I couldn't help but think about a dear sister/friend, Pastor Marilyn McClain. She would often invite us to her church, and we fellowshipped with her and her ministry for a while. One Sunday morning before I was to go out to speak, she called in the deacons and ministers for prayer. She asked me to stand in the middle of the prayer circle. She then asked James to pray for me. He got in the circle with me, took out his bottle of blessed oil, anointed me, laid his hands on me and prayed. The prayer was so powerful that we had church right there in her Pastor's Study. It was a powerful prayer! When he finished, we kissed. James, the other deacons and ministers went into the sanctuary. Pastor McClain and I stayed in her office. She was still getting her praise on. She said, "Sherry Bobbitt, I have never in my life heard a man, a husband pray like that for his wife. What a wonderful blessing. To God be the GLORY!!!" She continued getting her praise on. She said, after collecting herself, "Honey! Do you know how truly blessed that you are? It's not hard to see that he loves you and adores you but that type of praying for A spouse…that's special prayer on a spiritual level!" I told her that I was truly blessed because he prayed like that for me before I became his wife.

She asked James to render the altar prayer before she preached. Everybody was holding hands. Well Deacon Bobbitt rearranged the prayer circle before praying. Then he explained why. He told the congregation that he thought it was important for spouses to be holding hands and family members to do so as well. Then he prayed. It was a new experience for her members, but to this day, they have continued to pray that way.

After James passed away, Pastor McClain ministered to me concerning the prayers that she heard James praying for me…not what somebody told her, but what she heard for herself. He prayed boldly and unashamedly for his wife before other men. He was not ashamed to say that he was limited and how God was UNLIMITED to bless his wife beyond measures. She also reminded me that God and James have great expectations of me.

My husband wanted to leave a legacy; he wanted our marriage relationship to leave a legacy. I do believe that we have.

~POEM~

How blessed I am to have a man/husband who chose to keep me covered in such heartfelt prayers.
What a very special way to show me that he cares.

The first prayer that he prayed for me caught me by surprise because of the place.
It didn't matter where we were, seriousness was all over his face.

I never had a boyfriend that asked me to pray with him.
I truly had a very rare and precious gem.

That late evening was the beginning of many years of prayers to be prayed.
His dependency of God, through prayer, kept me covered like a huge tree that always rendered shade.

Love in a way that I never knew of, beginning to grow in my heart that night.
Without full understanding as to why he prayed the way he did, in my spirit it truly felt right.

From there we developed a prayer life together before becoming husband and wife.
We continued this journey until the last day of his life.

Bittersweet is the taste now in my heart because I can no longer hear him pray.
But all of the prayers that he prayed for me are in my heart to stay.

He was always unashamed to pray. Regardless of what others had to say in this area, he was seriously bold.
In spite of my feelings, I TRULY THANK God always missing him during prayer because I no longer have his hand to hold.

Author: Sherry E. (Jones) Bobbitt
My Song Choices: *Love Ballad* by L.T.D.
Night I Fell in Love by Luther Vandross
The Look in Your Eyes by Maize

CHAPTER 2: THE PRAYERS BEFORE I BECAME HIS WIFE

This is and always will be a very special prayer to me. I only heard a portion of this prayer; I say maybe somewhere in the middle of him praying. About three days before our wedding day, I woke up with James' hands on my chest and head. He was praying and crying. I didn't move or say one word. It was as if I couldn't if I wanted to.

His words were:

> LORD, I haven't had the greatest examples around me of what a Godly husband or a good husband should be. A part of me fears getting married because she seems to be so much more prepared than I am. Please allow her example as a Godly wife/good wife be that thing that I need to be the same to her. LORD, those things that she has talked to me about, those desires that she has had in her heart since she was a little girl, those dreams that she has had about being a wife, that it will please her husband, to never stop loving him, to never allow anyone to stand in her way to do all that she has deep within her to be as a wife. Surround her heart with wifely wisdom that only comes from you. Where she may be missing some things, and I don't believe that it is very much other than how to deal with me, please help her as you help me. Let the joy that she has never leave her heart when it comes to me. Please let her be forgiving because I know that I will make some mistakes, but I am not trying to. Please never let me do anything that may cause her heart to turn away from me. She has such great expectations for me. She calls me "Man of God" from time to time, even when I am getting

> high and that scares me because I am not who she says that she sees but I want to be. So whatever that is in her that sees and feels that, please don't let her loose it.

Well, that's all I remember because I fell back to sleep. The next morning, I woke up to breakfast cooking. As I sat up, there were flowers next to me and a note that just simply said "Just Because." I thought wow, just because. I went to the kitchen and did a little something, something. He smiled and said, "What up baby?" I said, "Just because." He said, "It's like that?" I smiled and walked back into the bedroom. What a wonderful brunch breakfast turned into because he followed me back to the bedroom.

We never explained or tried to explain any of our just because moments. So that he wouldn't ever try, I said one day, "Just because are moments in love and passion that don't need to be explained in words because the hearts understand what words may mess up trying to explain such enchanting intimate gestures." The beauty of just because is that it's never about birthdays, anniversaries, promotions, holidays or any special occasions. It's about when a special feeling comes in the heart which leads you to doing something surprisingly unexpected just because you love the one that you are with. It's like the song by Teddy Pendergrass *It Feel So Good Loving Somebody When Somebody Loves You Back.*

I miss James singing that song to me. There was no one sided love with us. Our special just because moments were something very special in our marriage relationship. They were one of the things that we both often prayed would never end in our marriage and they never did.

I would wish that I could have heard the rest of this prayer but, again, I took it as one of those times that all of it wasn't my business – just a matter between him and God.

The night before we were married, some of his friends had a bachelor party for him. We planned not to see each other after 8:00 p.m. A very dear friend of mine, Trice Anderson, and her baby came to spend the night with me. She helped me with my little last-minute things to do while the baby slept. About 10:00 p.m. there was a knock at the door, and it was

James. I went to the door, but I didn't open it at first. I asked him what he wanted. He said, "Baby, I just need to see you one more time." I went out on the porch but didn't turn the light on even after he asked me to. He had been drinking and he wanted to pray with me. I started to tell him no, but I didn't. He said,

> "I just had to see and talk to Miss Sherry Evonne Jones one more time. I'm in love with her and I just need her to love me the same and more when she becomes Mrs. James Lynn Bobbitt – Mrs. Sherry Evonne Jones Bobbitt. Are you going to change on me? You promised that as my wife you would do more. Can I count on you to be a good wife?"

I said, "Yes honey, no worries…happy wife, happy life. Now are you ready to pray and return to your party?" His prayer was:

> LORD, you know that I have been drinking but I need for us to pray, everything that I have asked you for concerning this diamond in the rough and me, I really mean what I have prayed about, I am really serious because I love her. I am in love, and I don't care who doesn't want us to be together. Keep us in YOUR LOVING CARE because we really don't know about marriage. We just want to be together right. Mamma Mary said that I must do right by her. She believes that I will be a good husband and so does Sugar Britches. I just need for you to always be with us, even in times of trouble, please be with us.
>
> LORD, I don't know what the future holds, but we have asked YOU for a long life together—me in my 80's and Sherry in her 70's. I just want this to be one of the happiest days of her life. I want to be her dream, her fairy tale and so much more than she has dreamed of, so much more. I want the sound of her voice to always be the one

> thing that can calm me down. Please let her continue, as we continue to be a comfort for each other. This will be my wife, yes, my wife LORD; my only wife and this she can count on. This is a promise, a promise that I will keep. Please let her be the last that I see when my time comes, her voice be the last that I hear and the touch that I feel. As she takes this leap of faith with me into the unknown, let her have no fear. We really don't know how to be husband and wife, but we know that YOU will be there with us every step of the way. I just had to come pray with Sherry. Please look pass me, the fact that I have been drinking. I just know that I couldn't rest until we prayed together one more time. In JESUS Name! AMEN! AMEN! AMEN!

We kissed and he said, "Good night, Sherry Jones." I said, "Good night, James Bobbitt. Try and have a good time at your party. I will be right here ready to become Mrs. James Lynn Bobbitt with bells on."

When I went back inside, Trice asked me what was wrong. I told her he wanted to pray and tell me goodbye. She asked, "Has he been drinking, what does he mean goodbye?" I told her that he said, "he fell in love with Miss Sherry Evonne Jones, and he wanted to make sure that she would still love him, and be in love with him, when she becomes Mrs. James Lynn Bobbitt, (Mrs. Sherry Evonne Jones Bobbitt) on tomorrow." Trice started laughing and said, "He is so in love; I've never seen James Lynn like this before and I've known him all my life." I told her that we prayed, and I told him to go try to enjoy his party. We opened a bottle of wine and picked up where we left off.

It is always a blessing to me when sharing my stories to have someone bear witness to what is being said. I will always cherish Trice being with me on the night before my wedding day.

Before I went to sleep, I couldn't help but think how many men have left their bachelor party to come pray with their wife to be? I simply smiled myself to sleep.

What an amazing feeling I had when I woke up the next morning, somehow in my heart I could feel James praying for me and I started praying for him. I choose to believe that we needed this prayer together before marriage.

~POEM~

James prayed for me before I became his wife.
He left his bachelor party concerning us and our married life.

We had promised not to see each other until our wedding day,
Apparently, this was so heavy on his heart, he had to come back and pray.

At first, I was kind of upset because I didn't want him to see me,
When he explained himself, I felt that it just had to be.

I turned off the porch light, opened the door, stepped out on to the porch and he took me by my hand.
He said, "My bachelor party will still be going on when I get back, tomorrow you will be my wife and I will be your husband.

We held hands there in the dark, kissing with our tears touching becoming one flow.
I felt as if I were in a fairy tale with my emotions giving off such a radiant glow.

He began to pray, thanking God for what was about to take place for us,
I thought how beautiful is this he just placed us in God's HANDS and said,
"It's YOU LORD for our Marriage that we will always trust."

He ended with how blessed he felt, and he hoped that I did to.
I said, "I feel exactly the same because I am so in love with you!

After Amen, he began to sing *It Feels So Good to Love Somebody That Loves You Back*. I love You soooo much.

We kissed again, his hands moving down my back with such a loving touch.

He walked off the porch, turned back and said "Goodbye Sherry Jones. I really want you to stay a part of my life."
I looked at him and said, "As long as I get to keep my boyfriend, James, you will never have to worry where Sherry Jones is. She will be very much a part of your wife."

I don't know how well he slept that night because for me it felt like a wink.
I was excited and nervous soon to be his bride, draped in pearls, pretty in pink.

Author: Sherry E. (Jones) Bobbitt
My Song Choices: *I Love You* by The Whispers
Lovin You by The O'Jays

CHAPTER 3: THE PRAYER AFTER THE WEDDING/BEFORE THE HONEYMOON

I never expected James to rush me away for prayer because the pastor prayed. Well, it was always like James to do the unexpected. As soon as we were introduced as Mr. and Mrs. James Lynn Bobbitt, we kissed and he whispered, "We need a moment alone Mrs. Bobbitt." We walked around to the side of our home. First, he said, "Hello Mrs. Sherry Evonne Jones Bobbitt. I will never forget this day and how I feel. We need to pray." I just smiled with tears. He took me by my hands, kissed the marriage hand, as he called it, and prayed. With tears rolling down our faces, he prayed,

> LORD, I am so happy, my heart is filled with joy today. I have a wife and she has a husband. We have made a huge step today. We really need you now more than ever. We are no longer just living together, we are living together right, and we THANK YOU, LORD! Let our marriage, our love, our relationship be so much better than we've dreamed of. Let our love never die, but only grow with each day that YOU bless us with. Please let our smiles always melt each other's hearts. Wow! In my wife's words 'LORD, I'm feeling groovie and like a fairy tale.' Shortly we will be going on our honeymoon. Please give us traveling mercies to Nashville and back. Let our wedding night be beyond her expectation and mine too. LORD, we THANK YOU!! It's the THREE of us from now on. Bless us as ONLY YOU CAN! We pray this prayer by faith in the precious name of JESUS!! AMEN! AMEN! AMEN! AMEN!

I was truly in the clouds at this point. As we were kissing after the prayer, my Uncle Mac came to the side of the house where we were. He yelled, "Man can't you wait until the honeymoon?!"

My brother, Tick (Ronald Jones), videoed our wedding. He followed our Uncle Mac. That part is on tape but sometimes now, I wish that the prayer after marriage was recorded. We all laughed, then James and I went to greet our guests.

I often wonder just how many married couples go off to themselves to pray after they are married...especially how many believers, saved married couples. I wonder because we weren't saved at the time, we hadn't properly committed our lives to Christ.

What a beautiful last Saturday in October. It was perfect weather for an outside wedding. Family and friends all gathered to see us pledge our love – to become Mr. and Mrs. James Lynn Bobbitt. In spite of there being a few who didn't want to see this day, I was basking in our prayers/my prayers being answered God ALLOWED it to happen and that was all that mattered.

We have so many wonderful memories from our wedding day. Not only do we have the video from my brother, we were also gifted pictures from our godfather/uncle, Bill Holt.

The party was over, the yard cleaned, bags packed...honeymoon was the next thing. I fell asleep on the way to Nashville but woke up while he was praying for me. I only remember him saying, "LORD, I am so happy, and I will do my very best not to let YOU or my wife down and if, by some unwanted reason that I do, will you both please forgive me and keep loving me." I didn't open my eyes or move; I just went back to sleep because that conversation was between God and James. The next thing I heard was, "Mrs. Bobbitt we're in Nashville, wake up Sugar Britches." I said, "Husband, get ready. I want to love you like you've never been loved before." He said, "WHAT?!" I responded, "You've been getting girlfriend love; you don't know nothing about the wife loving. He smiled and said, "Alright Mrs. Bobbitt." That night has always been like yesterday for us when we would talk about it. It was definitely a night to remember. Let's put it this way – I was drunk in love and woke up with the sweetest love Hangover. Ok!!

~POEM~

Many people don't believe in love at first sight, it can't be real.
Because you were not us, we didn't allow anybody to depict to us how we should feel.

The first time we were face to face, he said, "Girl, I love you",
I didn't say it back, but I was feeling the same way too.

I knew in my heart that I was looking at my husband and I nearly started to cry.
When he touched my hand I was on such a strange high.

If I surrendered to my feeling, we could have slept together that night and I didn't even know his last name.
Behind that thought I felt no shame.

So, on our first date I got more than my heart's desire.
Not only did he make love to me, he told me that I was going to be his wife and that set my soul on fire.

The next morning, he called me Mrs. Bobbitt then said, "I need to get used to it.
Because in his heart we were a perfect fit.

Finally, our wedding day came
It was official, I had a new last name.

Author: Sherry E. (Jones) Bobbitt
My Song Choices: *The Lady in My Life* by Michael Jackson
A Night to Remember by Shalamar

CHAPTER 4: THE FUNNY PRAYER

This was a time that I will never ever forget. James and I went to Pittsburgh, PA to visit our sister/friend Sherry Goodlow. We were very excited to take this trip because it was a first for both of us. It was beautiful all the way, many stops just to see things that we've never seen before and finally we made it to Pittsburgh, the home of his beloved Pittsburgh Steelers. We arrived early. Sherry was still at work, so we had lots of time to see the city. After a while we were ready to eat. James said, "Sugar Britches, wherever you want to eat, that's where we will go." I asked him if he was willing to try something different and he said yes, so we went to a Japanese place. When we got inside it was absolutely beautiful, with some soft jazz playing which was just perfect for me. He thought the place was very nice too.

The hostess came over to welcome us and seat us, next a waitress came to give us menus and to take our drink order. We started with iced tea with lemons. After a few minutes, two other couples were seated with us. They were all very nice and friendly. We all gave our orders, and the chef came out. He was doing his thing before and while preparing the food. Well, my man is from the country, as I would say brown hen house eggs country, James noticed the chef was missing some fingers. Then he said, "Hey, you be careful fixing my food; I don't need to see one of your fingers on my plate." Everyone at the table, including the chef, laughed! James was very serious. He looked at me and said, "Hell, he got me nervous. I better not see fingers on the grill." Meanwhile, James wanted to try some sake, so a gentleman at the table recommended Ginjo-shu sake and we tried it. When the waitress brought it to the table, James thought that the bottle and glasses (Masu) were very small but after he tasted it, he said, "This stuff is Japanese Moonshine." Again, everyone is laughing. The waitress brings out the bowls of rice. James politely says, "Excuse me, you brought bowls of rice, but you didn't bring any butter and sugar." She explained to James that they don't normally serve rice with butter and sugar, but she would be glad to bring him some. All I could think at that moment is how much I love my man. So, now it is time for the chef to serve us and I never saw this coming. As the chef is serving, James says, "Hold up, wait a minute. You just can't give our food away without asking first." The chef explained what he was doing. James leaned over and said, "You better be glad that I love you so much, got me eating this little ass food. No wonder they are all little people, they eat like birds." I was glad that he found the meal tasty but just not enough. He chilled out and enjoyed the rest of our time there. Before he paid our bill, the chef brought us some more food because he wanted James to be full. We thanked him and left. When we got in the car, James said, "Baby that's what you like, you can eat it. Hell, I need real food." He pulled over to the nearest Burger King. He ordered two whoppers with cheese and a large shake. THEN he was full for the moment.

It was getting close to the time to meet Sherry. When we got to her, the first thing that he told her was about his Japanese experience. She was cracking up and then popped me on my hand. Sherry said, "Sis, whatever you do, don't ever take Bro to another restaurant where he can't get his tummy full." She just kept laughing!!

We, got in the car with her, went to see some more friends and then to dinner. Sherry made sure it was an all you can eat restaurant. After dinner, we went to check into our room and chilled for the night. As we were in bed holding hands to pray, James says,

> LORD, please forgive me today. I know that I complained about the Japanese food, but I just thought it would be more. Let me learn to appreciate and enjoy doing things with my wife like she does with me. I'm just country. She knows it and YOU do too. Help me to be a little bit boujee for my wife.

I looked at him and said, “Hush, just hush” and laughed out loud. That just tickled me so much I never knew that a prayer could be funny until then.

He said, “Let me make it up to you baby. Well, let’s just say that making up for it was worth every moment!! I woke up a very happy wife. Missing my man soooooooooooo much!!!

~POEM~

Prayer is never meant to be funny; it was just James's choice of words.
Simply being himself saying things in a way that I never heard.

Regardless of the way he spoke in his prayers, he was very serious in spite of sounding odd.
Truly an understandable prayer language with God.

I loved his ways of just being real talking to God just like father and son sitting at the table.
James would often say, I pray because God is ABLE!

There was not a day that went by that he didn't pray.
Even when life's downs came, he had much to say.

How sweet it was to me to stand, watch him pray and cry.
I found that so spiritually attractive so many times and I can't find words to express why.

I seem to always know when to enter his prayer space.
When I knelt down next to him before taking me by the hand while praying, he would touch me on my face.

I have to admit to laughing a few times during prayer with my man.
You may never but I'm certainly glad that God did UNDERSTAND.

Oftentimes, I have wondered and still wonder what God THOUGHT about our prayer life.
In my heart I believed that HE just considered it a beautiful language with and between HIM, a husband and a wife.

Author: Sherry E. (Jones) Bobbitt
My Song Choices: *Your Smile* by Rene and Angela
Love's Victory by Ronnie Laws

CHAPTER 5: THE PRAYER FOR MY SELF-ESTEEM

My life took an unexpected twist while I was a teacher at a school for mildly ill children. One day during their lunch time, I told one of the young men to get his belongings together because his grandmother was due to pick him up in 15 minutes for a doctor's appointment. She came a little early, and he was still getting himself ready to go. While she was waiting, she took out some Youth Dew by Estee Lauder and sprayed some on herself. Minutes later I felt a tightening in my chest. I couldn't get air in or out. I thought maybe I was having a stroke or a heart attack. I just started praying, "LORD, please don't let me die in front of my students. LORD, please." I couldn't seem to get anybody's attention to let them know that something was going on with me. All I remember was dropping to my knees. I could hear people talking and I could hear James talking to me, but I couldn't answer him. I felt so very tired, my body felt weighed down and it was hurting to breathe. I would sleep off and on not being able to fully wake up. I was afraid because I didn't know where I was and there was nothing I could do.

When I finally opened my eyes, I could only see darkness and a little light. I could hear this same voice that I heard before. As I opened my eyes, I could see a Caucasian man with a beard. He was talking to someone about me. I looked over toward the person holding my hand certain that it was James – at least I was hoping that it was. I said, "Honey what's going on, where am I?" James said, "Hey Sugar Britches, hey baby, you are in the hospital. You have been here for a few days, try not to talk." Then the Caucasian man introduced himself to me letting me know that he was a pulmonologist specialist and that he was glad to see my eyes open and being able to talk a little bit. He then said, "I need to ask you some questions and if you get tired just let me know." He wanted to know how long I had suffered with asthma, why did I use such a strong cologne and why I didn't have a pulmonary doctor. I explained to him what happened and that I hadn't had an asthma attack since I was in junior high school. He explained that I had a very severe asthma attack. I was so messed up I didn't realize that I had on an oxygen mask until I started coughing. At this point, my health just continued to decline. Every time I thought that I was doing better, I would have another asthma attack. In 2005 I had nine visits to the hospital and had to be admitted each time. I just couldn't seem to get well. The first Tuesday in September James had to rush me to the hospital, and I was there until December 31st 6:30 p.m. Three different times the doctor told James that I was not going to make it. I was placed on a ventilator for a while and my man was going through. Finally, I was off the ventilator, but still breathing hard. I remember Sherry Goodlow-Allen coming to Nashville to see me. She said that she could hear me breathing outside of the door to my room. If you know Sherry, then you know that she took out her oil and started praying. After she finished, she told me that James called her, and she had to come see me. I was kind of upset because I had to be given Solu-Medrol injections which caused me to blow up. I was gaining weight so very fast, unable to rest well, and I was looking bad (to me). My face was extremely swollen, and I was nervous all of the time. I didn't want visitors. Sherry said, "Girl shut up. You need these meds to keep you alive. Don't worry about the weight. You get well first. Stop focusing on the weight gain and focus on breathing better so you can go home and stay home and stop coming in and out of here."

The time came for me to go home but I didn't want to leave the hospital. I felt safe there because not many people could see me, and I didn't want to be seen. I knew people were going to look at me like damn what has she been eating? Just as I thought, the first time I went to a family gathering I could hear the whispers and one of James' cousins openly said, "Oh my goodness! Girl, I thought that I'd never see you big like this". My feelings were so hurt. I was already feeling very self-conscious. I never felt that way before. I was never mean to people because of their appearance. I was raised that way. Clarice Jones (my mom) would smack the taste out of your mouth about something like that. She would tell us that we have no idea why people look the way that they look. She wasn't having that from us. I didn't tell James what was happening because he was having such a good time with his family and friends that he hadn't seen in a while because of my ongoing illness. I kept it to myself, getting deeper and deeper in a hole.

I got to a place where I no longer showered with him or let him see me naked. Sex was always in the dark. Finally, one day he had enough. One day I was waiting until he went to the store to take a shower, but he didn't go to the store. He parked up the street, walked home, came in the house, took my robe and all of the towels out of the bathroom. When I discovered that he did this I just started crying, begging him to bring everything back, but he refused. I stayed in there for about an hour, and he still wouldn't bring me anything to cover up with. He opened the door and said, "Enough is enough. Explain to me why I can't look at my wife anymore. Explain to me why you won't dress and undress in front of me anymore. Explain to me why I can't even make love to you by candlelight anymore. Baby you need to talk to me." I looked at him crying. He took me by the hand. As we walked into the bedroom, I saw that every light was on. I started crying and screaming. He was crying too but for a different reason. I yelled out,

> Look at me; hell look at me! I weigh nearly 400 pounds. I am on steroids. I keep getting bigger. I don't look the same, I don't feel the same and you can't possibly be enjoying me looking like this! Don't lie to me. I know that you know that people are making comments. That shit hurts my feelings because I wouldn't do that to anybody. I hate to eat in front of people. I hate to visit people that tell me where to sit or have people to have to get up because I can't squeeze through. Do you know how this makes me feel? No, you don't! I have to look like this to stay alive and I'd rather be gone."

James said,

> Mrs. Bobbitt the day I got the phone call from the school, and it was Amber telling me that they were waiting on the ambulance to come to get you, that scared the hell out of me. When I got to the school, they were bringing you out. You weren't responding to me. I followed them to the hospital. I waited, waited and waited until a doctor came out to tell me that you didn't have a stroke or heart attack. They said you had an asthma attack, and they were waiting on a pulmonologist specialist to come in because you were in critical condition. Hell, I never heard of a doctor like that and damn sho couldn't say the word. When he got there, he explained to me what was going on with you, what he had to do to try to get you out of the critical state that you were in, the meds that you would have to be on, the side effects and infections that came alone with it, and possibly you getting pneumonia. Hell, you gaining weight was the last thing on my mind and is not a concern for me now because, Sugar Britches, you are still here with me. How many times do I have to tell you that I can't live without you? You laying there and I couldn't do one thing but pray and wait. My prayers have been answered. Baby, first things first – your breathing to get better so you can get off the meds and then the weight issue if it's going to be an issue for you. I don't give a damn what nobody says. Yes, you are a big girl now but you a fine ass big girl. Why do you want to leave me? I love you. I have waited a long time for you to get this healthy where we are not in the hospital all of the time. Baby, you're gorgeous. One day you will lose the weight and I know who hurt your feelings. I told her yes, my baby is a big girl now. She can lose the weight when

she is all better, much healthier but you're going to die with that face. My baby still fine.

He began to kiss me everywhere, touch me everywhere. He turned on some music, got the baby oil, rubbed me down and made love to me. The next day he prayed for me.

When I got up, he was praying. When he finished, he asked me to come into the living room. He said, "Good morning, Sugar Britches. How do you feel? I need to pray for you, please." I said, "Good morning honey. I am so sorry…I just felt like I would be losing you soon because you loved my body the way it was. You couldn't keep your hands off me, always wanting to do me like you do.

He said, "I still do but it bothers me when you get short of breath. I still want you. I need you but I want you well enough to have me. I don't want you needing a breathing treatment after me loving on you. I am not trying to rush things because I'm going to need you there for me." He took me by my hands, kissed them and prayed.

FATHER! FATHER! I come right now as humble as I know how with a heavy heart because I can't seem to get my beautiful wife to understand that I love her now more than ever. LORD, YOU know exactly how I felt, how many times I cried out to YOU when the doctors wanted to give her up – when they said it was nothing else that they could do, my heart was crushed. So, I lift my beautiful, sexy wife up to you right now, asking for YOU to touch her heart, her mind and her soul. Speak to the spirit inside of her that hears YOU. Bring her back to life mentally, spiritually and physically. Restore her confidence, give her a 'brand new' self-esteem. Give her new joy, new peace. Please, let her see a new me, the me that can't survive without her, the me that sincerely, sincerely can't, cannot live without her. Open the eyes in her heart so she can see how I see her, and it doesn't

> matter what and how anybody feels about her or us. Bring her back to the things that she encouraged and keeps encouraging me with. Please take the shame away. None of this is her character. The devil is trying to mess with her mind because she is still a force to be reckoned with. He is just trying to find a way to keep her down since he couldn't take her out. As she lays down to rest later on today, rest upon her with YOUR LOVE and HEALING POWER. She is one of YOUR CHOSEN ONES. Allow her to rise above naysayers. LORD, if she did it during our hurricane season, surely, surely she can do it again and again if necessary!
>
> Let her walk and stand big, bold and beautiful and I am not talking about her size. Let her continue to walk in a room where plans were for her to fall but instead, she walks in like it's a platform. I need SHBOBB to do what she does LORD!! ONLY YOU can manifest these things that I am asking for in THE MIGHTY NAME OF JESUS CHRIST YOUR ONLY BEGOTTEN SON, IN HIS NAME I PRAY. AMEN! AMEN! AMEN!

I said AMEN too.

This was the second time that I had a deep moment. The first was when I lost our baby girl, J'Meese. James insisted that we get dressed and go to lunch. He took me downtown to The Standard. Linen tablecloths and napkins…he knew exactly what to do. We went for a walk in the park, stopped for ice cream on the way home and – let me just put it like this – the next morning ice cream never made it to the refrigerator because I was the bowl.

THE PRAYERS THAT HE PRAYED FOR ME

~POEM~

Seasons change in life; we find ourselves unprepared to stay on the journey that somehow becomes dark.
Often left wondering where is God, feeling like a little lost child left in the park.

Things going well then suddenly the clouds get between you and the sun,
Finding yourself in a place of "it is what it is" with nowhere to run.

Caught in a dust storm unable to see,
Trying hard not to feel like woe is me.

Strangely you're presented the path of unwanted pain,
The situation now moving like a runaway train.

Off in the distance you can see the sun once again,
Strength gained as the storm is about to end.

Without rhyme or reason there is no explanation for what you've gone through,
Once again, just picking up the pieces and doing what you got to do.

Sometimes the rules of life don't seem fair,
In spite of it all you still find it necessary to bow down on your knees for prayer.

Tough things are easier to go through when you have somebody to pray with and pray for you,
The beauty is the love that's within their heart does what's best without understanding too.

Author: Sherry E. (Jones) Bobbitt
My Song Choices: *Just the Way You Are* by Barry White
Perfection Combination by Stacy Lattisaw and Johnny Gill
In The Mood by Tyrone Davis

CHAPTER 6: PRAYERLESS MOMENTS

Wow! I know that you may be wondering what does prayerless moments mean? Well, through our story, hopefully you will understand what I mean by this.

A prayerless moment for us was when we couldn't put words together to pray, especially during heated moments between us. Moments when you both are pissed off, hot as fish grease, when enough is enough and more words said will make matters far worse. You know, THAT upset.

You both realize that you really need to pray, certainly in great need of prayer but your present mindset just won't come into compliance. You both are deep in your feelings, truly feeling some kind of way and trying hard not to say or do anything that you will regret.

You may call these moments something else or you may be one of those couples who never go through. That wasn't us. We called them prayerless moments and we took out time apart for self-examination when these moments occurred.

This is one prayerless moment for us that we never forgot and shared it when talking to other couples. Nothing! Nothing! Nothing but God and plenty of prayer in advance keeps you together during moments like these because the enemy and a few folks really want to see married couples apart and at odds with each other.

One morning I woke up to get ready for work. I sat up, turned on my lamp, looked over, there James was sitting up. I said, "Good morning honey."

Well, he just went in about a situation that I assumed that we were good on. Apparently, he spent a lot of time during the night getting all over charged about the situation. I said, "James, I really thought that we reached an understanding." His reply was, "Well I just been thinking." To which I replied, "I really don't have the energy for this. I have a classroom today with three students that have Tourette's Syndrome. Let's not do this, we did this last night." Normally, I would act as if he was not speaking at all but this time, I went right there with him. I wasn't having it, not that day. We fussed the entire morning but still doing what we normally did getting ready for work. I fixed our breakfast and lunch for the day. He took the trash out, started my car, turned on the AC, yet we were still fussing. We walked out together. He walked me to my car; we kissed but kept fussing.

Now, I am telling God all the way to work about his son and how this time I guess that God would have to check both of us because now I am very upset. As soon as I got to work, he called my classroom, and we fussed over the phone. I hang up and then we went to the mad texting stage. Finally, that ended when he had to start working. I was having the day from hell with my students. I was so looking forward to my lunchtime, plus I had an extra hour to chill because it was Outside Resource Day. Yeah, I didn't have to be in the gym with the students. Wishful thinking. Five minutes into my lunch time, my phone rings in my classroom – it was James. I didn't answer so he called my cell phone. Then my classroom phone again. I answered but said nothing, so he said nothing. We said nothing for about 15 minutes and finally he said, "I am mad at you Sherry Bobbitt." I said, "I am very upset with you Mr. Mean Jeans." He said, "Oh now you are that mad that I have to be Mr. Mean Jeans today?" I said "yes", and he said, "well bye" and I said "bye" and we hung up. My day was really going south, and I began fleecing after some relief. Finally, the workday was over. I was feeling like a new woman driving home. I did not want to deal with Mr. Mean Jeans. I was done. I really didn't care if he was late getting home that evening. As I went inside, it didn't feel like my little love cottage. I sat on the sofa and cried. I was that upset, feeling like if I could just sit there alone on the sofa and vent that I would feel better afterwards but that didn't get to happen. Wouldn't you know it, Mr. Mean Jeans was pulling up. I wiped my tears, put on my big girl attitude getting ready for whatever. He came in rushing to the bathroom, said nothing, just looked at me. When he came out, he looked at the mail, went to the kitchen, got a bottle of water, sat on the sofa next to me, started drinking the water and passed me the bottle. I took a small sip and passed it back. He put the bottle down. We sat there quietly – saying nothing to each other. After the sun set, we were still sitting on the sofa together. He put his hand on top of mine, pulled it toward his lips kissing my hand, the one he called The Marriage Hand. I burst into tears. He cried too. We hugged each other for a while, then he put his arms around me, and I laid my head on his chest. The next thing I knew it was morning, a new day. I was thinking, please no fussing today. He was already awake. He said, "Good morning, Sugar Britches." I replied, "Good morning, Mr. Mean Jeans." He said, "Damn, I'm still Mr. Mean Jeans? What can I do to be Big Daddy?" I just looked at him with tears falling. He said, "Honey, I love you, too."

As he picked up his phone, our conversation continued:

James: I know that you are hungry, your tummy has been talking. You probably didn't eat yesterday.

Me: No, I didn't.

James: Let's ride to Kentucky and spend the day.

Me: No, I don't want to go anywhere.

James: Sugar Britches, then what do you want to do? Whatever you want, I will do it.

Me: Go take off those Mean Jeans and meet me in the shower.

Smiling, James said, "Ok, if that what you want, I said, "It's what I want." So, we went together to take a shower. We just stood there for a while holding each other. Well, what happened from there was a little something, something, ok. We oiled each other down which led to passionate intimacy. We ended up sharing a big bowl of cereal, watched the Cowboy Network Channel, and fell asleep.

I woke up to my phone ringing. It was him calling me. I turned over to find he wasn't there. He was calling me from the car wash. Our conversation was:

James: Hi, can I please talk to my girlfriend?
Me: Hi, this is she. I'm so glad that you called me.
James: I want to take you out. Will you ride to Memphis with me?
Me: Yes, I will be ready when you get here.

I got up, took a shower, packed our luggage, got all dolled up, called him to tell him that I was ready. He was on the porch, so I told him to come get our bags. He did, we went to Memphis, had a wonderful time.

We never talked about that situation again. It seemed as if it never happened, if you can understand that. I really enjoyed my boyfriend that weekend and he really enjoyed his girlfriend. I mean **really, really**, ok!

Sometimes, I felt that we didn't have to try to explain "why" all of the time because sometimes you really don't know why. Things just happen, get out of hand and all you can try to focus on is finding your way back to Love Land. At least that was my take on it, which became his, too. He prayed prayers for moments like this and I did too. Truly the power of prayer doing what we couldn't do, refused to do, at that moment.

Before James passed away, we talked about some of those moments like this one…how we really couldn't remember what actually started those moments of being so upset with each other, but we never forgot how they ended. That night in the hospital as we were lying in bed, we just THANKED God. James thanked me for always wanting the simplest things to do to get us back to a good place in our marriage relationship. What a beautiful time it was reflecting together. I did not realize that it would be our last time doing so.

I am left with sweet memories and blessed to share some of our story as was his desire. As I am typing this chapter, I recall telling him, "Well, you know that if I do honor your request to use my gift of writing to write what you want to share about us, there will be people who will say that she is making this up." He replied,

> Well, hell that's on them and what they choose to believe. It's all good. The three of us know exactly how

> true this is – you, me and God. We just need for you to write. Baby, I have told you over and over again, for years, that you should write books. Don't let me down, even if I may not be with you when you do but I will always be in your heart when you do. I am so proud of you, and most of all proud that you gave me your hand in marriage. I know that I have acted a damn fool, but you loved me anyway. You will be writing our stories, your poems and any other things that God BLESSES you to write. I know who you are…I just wished that you did. One day you will.

As, you can see that I am. My prayer is that one of our prayerless moments has been inspiring, a teaching moment and most of all a tool to use.

SHERRY E. (JONES) BOBBITT

~POEM~

Prayerless moments were a part of us,
From the beginning of our relationship and in our marriage, it was in God where we placed our trust.

In those ugly moments when needless thoughts and words got in our way,
We still kept fleecing after loving and meaningful things to say.

We asked God to always check us when we were wrong,
Also, to saturate our hearts, minds and souls with ONLY HIS POWERFUL LOVE SONG!

We truly believed that God would always clear away all of the debris from dangerous storms that unexpectedly blew in,
Always keeping us mindful that we weren't only husband and wife, but we were also lovers and friends.

Trouble at its finest would sometimes find a way in but it couldn't stay,
I know that we survived because we sought God together every day as we held hands on bended knees to pray.

Making up was one of those special things that we loved to do, which most of the time brought us both to tears,
Emotions emerging through the dark cloud that was formed to keep us apart, but our moments always left us toasting with cheers.

Sometimes we bite our own lip or even poke ourselves in the eye,
Determined to continue the journey together never getting caught up in asking why.

I just loved how we never returned to the scene of the crime,
Only clinging to the strength that love provided with our hearts making music like a bell chime.
Each other knowing the right spots to touch,
Anger simply vanishes because we always needed each other very much.

Our prayerless moments left us many times blinded to the right things to do,
To God Be the GLORY for ALWAYS pulling us through.

Author: Sherry E. (Jones) Bobbitt
My Song Choices: *Just Because* by Johnnie Taylor
Don't Mind by Mary J. Blige

CHAPTER 7: THE PRAYER FOR LIFE, LOVE AND JOY TO BE RESTORED

I went through a season in my life feeling worthless as a wife and woman. During that time, I felt lifeless. From the age of five, I have always wanted to be a wife and mother. The day that we found out that we were going to have a baby was one of the happiest moments in our lives. I used to play on a lady's softball team for the company that I was working for at the time. I got sick one evening. Naturally, I assumed that it was because it was so hot that day. James took me to the doctor's office the next day.

I was hit by a motor bike as a child, so the chances of me getting pregnant were slim according to the doctors back then but it happened! I was pregnant! Unfortunately, an unexpected turn of events took place. Early one morning, I started cramping extremely bad. I could not move or make a sound; I could only cry and pray. Suddenly I opened my eyes to see a beautiful, dark chocolate little girl standing right beside my bed. She had a dark complexion like James. She also had his eyes, but she looked like me. She was a very pretty little girl. She said, "Hi mommy. Don't cry, it will be alright. You are going to have to let me go and I will be alright. I love you both." She stood there smiling with teeth just like James. That made me smile and cry. When I tried to reach out to touch her, she seemed to fade away and my cramping grew worse. I woke James up crying. He asked what was wrong and did I wet the bed? When he pulled back the bedspread, I was bleeding. He hurried to put on his clothes, helped me to put mine on, and off to Jackson we went. James was speeding and a State Trooper stopped us. When he got to the car, he bent down to talk to James. As he looked over at me, he could see the blood on the towel. He told James to turn on his flashers and follow close behind him. After we arrived at the hospital, my doctor was called. I was rushed to surgery and what happened in that operating room turned my world upside down. When I woke up, I never opened my eyes. James was lying next to me. I grabbed his shirt crying and yelling. I knew that she was gone. Nobody had to tell me that our precious little life was no longer living inside of me. I told James that I was sorry that I lost our baby girl. He told me that it wasn't my fault, and we can try again. Soon the doctor came in. Realizing that I knew about the baby, he stood by my side and told us that he had to give me an emergency hysterectomy – a complete hysterectomy! I felt like my heart fell out of my chest onto the floor. James had just told me when I healed that we would try again but that wasn't going to happen—ever. I was crushed. My mind could not wrap around the news. I was already devastated, but the report from the doctor was like throwing salt in my fresh wound.

The doctor prayed with James and me, then left the room. We cried, cried and cried. Finally, the nurse came in. My blood pressure was high, so she gave me some shots for the pressure and the pain. Before I drifted off to sleep, I told James to go home and throw away the clothes that he had on because there was blood still on him. He said, "Baby, I'm not going anywhere until you go to sleep. You really need some rest, and I will be back before you wake up." We kissed, he sat in the chair next to the bed holding my hand and that's all I remember because I went to sleep.

I woke up in severe pain. I buzzed for the nurse. James had been asleep but woke up as she came in. She gave me more pain meds. James comforted me with constant kisses and back to sleep I went.

Apparently, he did go home, changed clothes and came back. When I woke up, it was the next day, a new day with the same hurt in my heart. James was asleep in the chair. I looked at him and cried. I felt that I was no longer enough woman for him; there would be no children that were ours, none. I couldn't pray. I felt as if there was nothing to pray for because what was done could not be undone. I was worthless, only good for sex is how I was feeling. I cried myself back to sleep and when I woke up James was lying next to me. He told me how he didn't want me to feel but it was too late. I was already feeling that way.

Well, it was time to go home, get back to life—a life that I no longer knew how to live at the time. I simply stayed in the house. I did not talk to anyone, not even my own mother. I barely talked to James. I didn't eat very much, just a few bites to take my meds. One evening, I asked James to help me get in the tub. While I was waiting for him to bring me a pillow to sit on in the tub, I noticed that I really looked bad. I looked as if I was strung out on drugs, and I did not like that and I just started screaming. James rushed back and held me until I calmed down. We got in the tub together and just sat for a while. James got me ready to lay down and rest. He went to Momma Mary's (his grandmother) to get some dinner. She made some chicken n dumplings. I didn't eat much but I was glad to see James have a wonderful meal. I was no longer doing anything, not even cooking.

That night James prayed from the depths of his soul. He prayed for my return, for me to come back to God, for me to come back to him but, most of all, for me to come back to myself. I could see his lips moving but there were times that I couldn't hear him. I seem to be floating, really wanting to die while he was praying. Later that night he said:

> You started crying and screaming but I kept praying for you. I kept praying even after you went to sleep. I placed you in God's HANDS. I can't fix this. I don't know what else to do, I have been right here. I tell you all of the time that I love you. I tell you every day that I wasn't marrying you based on you having my children. I am taking care of you the best that I know how. Can't you see that I am hurting too? No, I didn't carry her inside of me like you did but she was inside of me too. Hell, that was my seed—my seed of love in love. You didn't get that life without me, so no, I don't know what that feels like to never have a child because I do have a son, but this has hurt me more than you know. I have been here for you, but you haven't been here for me like you are the only one hurting. Sugar Britches I am hurting too, I am.

My heart broke in a different way that night. I was hurting him, and I couldn't see it because I was so blinded by my own hurt. That night all of that came to an end. James never had the experience again. I never let him hurt again; I was totally there for him from that point on.

The next day he went to work, when he got home, his Sugar Britches cooked dinner. I overdid it, up on my feet too much to the point I began to hurt. I was sleep when he got home. When I woke up, he was asleep next to me in the bed. At first, I wondered if he had eaten. When he passed gas, I knew then that he had, and I went back to sleep.

I did not get to hear that prayer; not very much of it. I only heard him saying, "LORD PLEASE, LORD, I need you to help me know how to help my wife through this. I need my wife. Our baby girl is gone and only YOU know why. LORD, I can't anymore." That's just about all that I heard because of the state of mind that I was in. What I do know is that my husband prayed for my return, and I did. Again, maybe I didn't need to hear all of it.

THE PRAYERS THAT HE PRAYED FOR ME

~POEM~

There once was a precious little life inside of me,
She was made from love being in love—a place where James and I chose to be.

The news of her coming brought the most beautiful unspeakable feelings in that season of our life,
I felt complete and whole my dreams were coming true; I was about to become a mommy and a wife.

Unaware of the evil that I was in the midst of, that was going to cause us much pain,
I was too busy enjoying the three of us dancing together in our own rain.

In a vision she came to me saying that she could not stay,
Suddenly I began cramping severely holding my tummy praying please don't let it end this way.

James rushed me to the hospital but there was nothing that they could do,
Not only did I lose our precious little baby girl, I had to have a complete hysterectomy too.

We cried together when the doctor explained the reason why,
My world was shattered, I couldn't believe that the precious little life inside of me had to die.

James watched for weeks as I was slowly slipping away,
He felt helpless but had the strength to keep me covered in his love praying for me every day.

Deeply wounded and blinded by my tears, sorrow had become my middle name,

My dreams had drifted so far away from me I couldn't recognize my surroundings because life wasn't the same.

I no longer wanted to get married because his love seeds would come inside me, but they would not grow,
James held me in his arms and promised that our love hadn't lost its glow.

Later in years we found out that I was a victim of an unnecessary hysterectomy then there was a different type of pain for us to bare.
Again, my man went into deep prayer but this time I was there to share.

Prayer was always a very big part of our life together,
The shelter of God's ARMS and James' Arms to keep me protected in some of life's stormiest weather.

Many, many years had gone by and she had stopped coming in my dreams,
but she did during a short nap before James passed away,
We were all in a beautiful garden together. They looked at me smiling moving toward the other side and for now I have to stay.

Our precious little girl now has one of us to hold her little hand,
Bittersweetly considering this to be The FATHER'S PLAN.

Author: Sherry E. (Jones) Bobbitt
My Song Choices: *Loving You* by The O'Jays
Ready or Not by After 7

CHAPTER 8: THE MARRIAGE HANDS PRAYER

I know that by now, some of these chapter titles may seem a bit strange but they were our word choices for the many different avenues and levels for our marriage relationship.

This all started when James came home with a Little Pocket Card that he found at a Hallmark store while doing some electrical work in the mall in Jackson, TN. We were married exactly one week when he got it. He said, "When he bought it, he noticed there was To: and From:. He smiled because it was the first time that he wrote the word wife, and it was official.

I was out shopping with my mom and little sister that day. When I got home, he was there. Before I got out of the car he was standing on the porch. He asked me if I had bags to which I replied, "I got it husband, I appreciate you, husband." He was holding the door open. As I walked in, we kissed. I said, "Thank you husband. I missed you too, husband." He just smiled that James Bobbitt smile—one that I will miss for the rest of my life.

Anyway, he wanted me to come into the dining room. As I walked in, I saw flowers, a teddy bear, some wine, strawberries, cream cheese, ready whip, and a card. I said, "Oh my, how surprisingly enchanting is this!" He said, "You and your way with words. My girl." He pulled out the chair for me to sit down and then he sat in front of me just smiling for a minute. Next, he said, "I want to pray for your marriage hand and our marriage hands." I said, "Ok." He took my left hand, placed his left hand on top of mine and said, "These are our marriage hands. These hands wear the wedding rings that were prayed over before we put them on each other by Rev. Clifford Martin, Sr. and it is now my place to pray over our marriage hands." I just smiled, bowed my head and closed my eyes.

His prayer was:

LORD, THANK YOU for blessing me with this precious hand in marriage. I am coming to you right now asking that I never forget how precious these hands are and how they were especially made for me to hold until death do us part. I really don't know how to care for such a wonderful blessing, but I know that YOU will lead and guide me. My granny told me that if I asked YOU that YOU would. So, I am asking YOU to teach me because if, for some ungodly reason, I do something wrong, please let her love for me never take this hand back. Bless it that it will always, always remember the day that she gave it to me because she loves me, in love with me…my gift of her love for me. When times come and she is upset with me, let her look at the marriage hand and find reason to forgive me and to keep on loving me. I know that I have been with many women before her, but their hands were never the right hand. Her hand is not just the right hand in marriage, it will be the ONLY hand in marriage for me. Let that hand comfort me in my most uncomfortable moments, ease my pain, get me to the point where I'm not frustrated so I can always seek YOU for whatever help I need when things go wrong. LORD, I don't want nothing to go wrong but when they do, I will always need YOU and my wife. Now bless our hands—the hands that are now one hand. I really don't know if I am making sense right now but LORD, YOU know my heart, what's been on my mind and what I am really meaning. Please let it all make sense to my wife so she can understand this prayer because I mean it not just from my heart but my soul too. I really need YOU for this moment, this prayer to be as special to my wife as it is to me. It may sound crazy, but please let it make sense to her, my wife/your child. Man, I'm not trying to be tripping; I am just trying to be right and stay right in this marriage.

Lifting up our hands, he said:

Bless this marriage, bless our hands. Do with them what we don't know how to do. Use them to cause us to always stay in love with each other, no matter how bad the storms may get. Let her hold on to YOUR HAND and my hand too because I need this so much. Sometimes I get scared because I don't ever want her to ever not be in my life. I have already made some mistakes and she gave me her hand in marriage anyway. She calls me Man of God, Priest of her household. I want to live up to what she sees and feels. LORD, I ask for these blessings in the MIGHTY NAME OF JESUS CHRIST! Amen! Amen! Amen!

I said, "Amen! Amen! Amen!" and we hugged. He asked me did I understand what he was praying for. I said, "Somewhat, and what I don't, I will…I promise. I will and I did!

The Little Pocket Card reads, "SHERRY Feminine 'Delight thyself also in the Lord; and He shall give thee the desire of thine heart.' Psalms 37:4" On the back of it in the TO space, he wrote "My Wife Sherry" From: James.

Exactly sixteen years later we were invited to a Valentine's Day conference for married couples at Olivet Missionary Baptist Church by Pastor Michael and Lady/Minister Freda Cousin. It was a very good conference, a different way to celebrate Valentine's Day. The guest speaker asked many questions and then she asked a question regarding having an item that their spouse gave them. No one had anything except me! Wow, nobody else had anything with them. Couples shared what special tokens of love they had, but those items were home. All of a sudden, it hit me, yes, I had something. I reached into my purse, pulled out my wallet, opened it, took out my Little Pocket Card and gave it to James. His eyes got so big and full of tears. We kissed. The speaker said, "Ok! What just took place over there? What do you all have?" James wanted me to tell her, but I said, "No. You tell it…after all you gave it to me."

After wiping tears, James explained that he had no idea that I still had the card. He said,

> "First of all, she keeps everything that I give her. She cherishes everything. I just didn't know that she carries this in her wallet. I gave this to her exactly one week after we were married. She came home to a one-week anniversary celebration/prayer. That's a whole story within itself, but I gave her this card. She promised to always keep it with her. Sixteen years ago, she put it in her wallet and apparently she has kept it in her wallet at all times as she promised. Ya'll just have to excuse me; this has blown me away.

The speaker blessed us with a love offering after the conference was over. She said that she had never been so moved before.

I still have my Little Pocket Card in my wallet. If there is to be another man in my life, the card must stay in my wallet and my prayer is that he will truly understand why it has to be. The night that James gave me My Little Pocket Card I remember saying, "LORD help me to understand his heart, always to be able to feel his heart no matter how far apart we may be and let me never lose this sweet little sentiment of my husband's love for me. In JESUS NAME! Amen! Amen! Amen!" I just said this little prayer in my heart before putting it in my wallet. Over the years, I have had many different wallets, but just like my driver's license it goes in there, too. We ended that night with intimacy on another level. We woke up in our bed fully clothed with our shoes on. He even still had his baseball cap on.

Before James passed away, we began worshipping with Pastor Mario Johnson who James and I called our son. The last Sunday that James was able to be in worship service he could hardly walk but he wanted to go to church. We were over an hour late. He was only able to make it to the last row and that's where we sat. Pastor Mario acknowledged us before he preached. This made James feel so special. Mario didn't say Deacon Bobbitt and Pastor Bobbitt. He said, "I praise God for you being able to make it to the house this morning Pop James and Momma Bobbitt. We both dropped tears. While Pastor Mario was preaching, James took me by the marriage hand, placed mine on top of his, took out his cell phone, then said, "I don't know if I will be able to be with you when our next wedding anniversary comes. I always wanted a picture of our marriage hands—a professional one—but this will have to do." He took a picture right there in church while Pastor Mario was preaching. We cried and held each other in church. He thanked me, once again, for my hand in marriage. I can't say what he was thinking but I was screaming in my spirit, LORD PLEASE, PLEASE LET US HAVE MORE TIME! After, James left me, I told Mario what was going on that Sunday at church.

Life is so strange sometimes. We plan, we believe, we have faith, we pray, and the opposite occurs.

~POEM~

Two left hands filled with something special just for us,
Hands that my husband chose to call the marriage hands that we placed into the ONE that we trust.

These hands didn't have any magic, but they were a special pair filled with our love,
It was if they were as one in an anointed glove.

James prayed over our marriage hands throughout our entire marriage, even on his last day,
The prayers were never the same, his words filled with such sweet sentiments always leaving me no words to say.

I never prayed over our hands, it was his special thing to do,
Each time that he finished, I only said, "Honey, I love you, too."

I still have the picture of our marriage hands in both of our phones, I even put it on my Facebook page,
Since he has been gone, from time to time I miss those hands and go into a crying rage.

Precious, our marriage hands will always be to me,
Stained in my heart is the placed that they will forever be.

God BLESSED our marriage hands with a special gift of love ever so sweet
We chose to believe that they were a symbol that made our marriage relationship complete.

Author: Sherry E. (Jones) Bobbitt
My Song Choices: *The Makings of You* by Curtis Mayfield
Here and Now by Luther Vandross

CHAPTER 9: THE PRAYER OF FORGIVENESS AND A CHANCE TO REDEEM HIMSELF {OUR HURRICANE SEASON}

I must say this, too, is a very difficult chapter and I did not realize it until it came to my heart to share. It was truly a time when I wasn't sure if we were going to make it as husband and wife. One thing I was certain of, however, during that unexpected, awful season of our life was that I could not fix my heart and mouth to say that I did not love James anymore. That left me feeling extremely foolish, with plenty of people surrounding me to make me feel even worse.

One may say why even include this chapter? I say, "Why not? It was very much a part of our story—one that we endured together, one that most married couples could not have survived, one that I must say that it was God's PLANS for us to stay together. We survived and came out stronger. There was nothing fake about it. We were truly stronger. If not, we could not have done all that we did as a married couple. We had love on a level that I did not know was reachable.

I cannot express the level of embarrassment to include this chapter in this book, but it was a part of our lives. It was not my intent to have this chapter, but many have told me that my healing will come from writing the book. Clarity will be a big part, giving me a different outlook and maybe see God's plan for my new journey in life.

Remember, this is OUR story, and we lived a loving life together after this horrific hurricane in our lives. Indeed, this hurricane season bent some branches on our tree, but we didn't break! We were able to stand, face whispers, people looking at us like we were crazy, family treating us differently, being temporarily homeless, spiritually hurt, not having many people in our corner encouraging us. We had people offering to give us money for a divorce but not to help us stay together. We were under an attack, but we chose to fight together and were genuinely blessed.

I am not looking for anyone to fully understand because there were times that I didn't understand myself. I just simply trusted God, my biological father (Tyrone Jones) and my husband James Lynn Bobbitt. Why? As I prayed seeking answers from God, I only kept hearing, "Be still and give this to me."

In the midst of it, this is what my father said to me:

> At first, I wanted to have James killed. When I talked to my best friend, Walter Johnson, he told me to pray because there was some great interference going on. He said to trust God through this situation, pray for your daughter, call your daughter and pray with her. Explain to her how she really should trust God to fix this, to turn things around. Encourage her to hold her head up. She is living in a small town; it sort of makes matters worse. She has to feel at her worse and, as her father, you don't need to make things any worse. In spite of how you feel Jones, don't lose her and let her get lost in this situation. I feel that God has something GREATER for James and Sherry.

To be honest I was looking for Hood Dad, St. Louis/East St. Louis Dad. (You have to be from there or know a little something about St. Louis/East St. Louis to understand Hood Dad but that was who I was expecting to hear from. Instead, I heard from a dad/father that I had never heard from before. It was the very first time that my pop ever prayed **for** me and **with** me. From this hurricane season in my life, my pop and I developed a different type of relationship together. We started praying and studying the word of God together. This was absolutely the beginning of a wonderful and new relationship for us. This brings me to tears to write this because I really miss bible study with my pop. He would always call me to study with him when he had a speaking engagement or when he was just seeking some understanding of the scriptures. It may sound strange to say, but that hurricane season brought and birthed so many wonderful times and memories in my life with my pop. I really can't help but cry right through this moment. Having my husband killed or hurt would have taken my pop away from me but praying with me and praying for me brought us to a level of love between a father and daughter that I never gave thought to. I am truly blessed in the "all things working together" part.

I am also extremely thankful and THANK God for Mr. Walter Johnson for being that vessel that God used to speak life and not death in a season that not only blessed my marriage relationship with my husband, but also in the development of a new level relationship with my pop. My pop is resting in peace now. As he was passing, I was able to be there holding his hand. My brother, Tick and I were there together for that moment.

Well… there is nothing to say about my brother Tick because he just didn't talk to me. He would call to see how I was doing but he didn't talk to me. This hurt me but it was what it was. I would be remiss not to mention my godfather, Bill Holt, bka Uncle Bill. He has been a part of my life from the very beginning. He and my parents lived in the same apartment building; he lived upstairs over them. I can't seem to recall important times in my life that Uncle Bill was not a part of it, including my hurricane season. Naturally, my pop called Uncle Bill to tell him what happened to me. They were both very upset but took basically the same view toward the situation after having sound wisdom poured into them. Uncle Bill called me at my mom's and simply asked me what I wanted to do. Did I want to stay to work things out or come home because he and my pop would come and move me back to St. Louis. I really could not put the words together to explain what was in my heart and on my mind because I was so hurt and confused about why it all happened in the first place. I finally answered Uncle Bill and said:

> "I don't know if you can understand this or not, but I am more emotionally hurt that I am physically hurt. It's like I can't turn the love off. I wish that I could turn the

> love off. It's as if I know exactly what happened because I was there but I can't believe he did this. It was like it was him but not him as if he was being used to hurt me. He even yelled out, 'Why am I doing this?!' I just don't know if I could TURN THE LOVE OFF!!!!!!!! I can easily walk away and never look back. Do you think that I am stupid because of all that I keep hearing from my mom and Keisha (my little sister)? They have one time to just put their arms around me and hug me. I really need a hug and I haven't gotten one yet.

Uncle Bill said, "You haven't had the chance to process this, and I can only imagine what you are going through. I love you and I will call to check on you tomorrow." He called the next day and told me that he was praying and had some friends praying too. Actually, that made me sadder because now more people knew about what happened.

It was natural for my mom to be upset but I felt that she lost sight on how much I needed her to hold me and let me cry. Instead, most days, she referred to me as being a stupid bitch, crazy as hell, dumb as they come and a few other phrases. To have this hurricane season, along with my mom acting so ugly toward me with so much anger, not talking to me, talking at me about me badly to others was salt in an open wound. I could hear her on the telephone talking about me. I felt totally abandoned. She never once prayed with me during that time, but she was still my mom, so I just let her be.

I never spoke up for myself. My spirit was being beat down in more ways than one. Before my mom passed away, she told me how wrong that she was for allowing me to go through such a trying time alone. She somewhat feared that I would try to get back at her for her behavior when she became paralyzed. I told her that all had been forgiven. I had never held it against her. Life was getting very short for her and I'd rather us enjoy each other while we could. We went from that moment with us just remembering all of the good times. The next day mom and James had a long private talk. I never asked them what it was about. All I know is they fell asleep holding hands and that truly brought joy to my heart.

Not having my mom and sister there for me made it worse. Yes, they were upset but in their rage they seem to have missed where I needed them to just hold my hand. YES, be mad, be upset but just hold my hand. Instead, they only had ugly words for me. It started with calling me stupid then escalated to calling me a stupid crazy bitch. I had nowhere else to go so I had to deal with it. I remember wishing that one of my sisters-in-law would come and see me one day. They did not show up or call. I felt so alone. I know that nobody really knew what to say but a little compassion would have helped. Finally, my little sister-in-law, Tracee, came to see me. She came in, sat down next to me, put her arms around me and cried. I ended up consoling her, but it was what I needed. She wanted to come sooner but didn't know whether I wanted any visitors or not. She finally determined that there was only one way to find out. I am so glad that she came because it was my first hug, a hug that did more for me than she will ever imagine. Finally, my mother-in-law came, and it was the most intense visit. She said nothing that made sense to me because it was nothing about how to fix the situation. She and my mom talked back and forth to each other about James and me as if I was not in the room. I had two moms in the room with me. All I needed from them was prayer, hugs and to tell me let's believe God that everything will be alright. I needed them to encourage me to hold my head up—something/anything encouraging, but they didn't. I was alone in the midst of this unwanted thunderstorm praying by myself.

My mom and I had our bumps and bruises, but she was and is still my mom. She eventually had a conversation with me about that season. About a week before she passed away, she asked me to forgive her. She talked about how James' life turned around and that, never in a million years, would have believed that he would be the "best Sunday School teacher" she ever had, how GOD had a purpose and a plan. She was glad that I didn't listen to her. After that conversation, she prayed for me. She held me and prayed for me! In her prayer she asked God to

> Keep his loving arms around me when James' time came. She knew that I would be the big girl that she expects when her time came, but James leaving me would be a different loss and she wouldn't be around to help me. I wouldn't have her to talk to.

She added, "Hold her together so she can grow and teach from her experience because I expect that you will use her Lord in that way." I cried in my mother's arms. She was partially paralyzed so she placed one arm around me. I placed the other arm around me so she could fully hold me for the last time.

The last week of her life she suffered a very bad stroke leaving her unable to speak and she was totally paralyzed. I would sit talking to her and was wondering if she could hear me. The nurse told me that she did. The nurse said, "Ms. Jones only opens her eye when she hears your voice." I began to notice. Before I was in tears talking to her trying to prepare myself for her passing. Keisha was with me the afternoon that mom passed away. I was looking out of the window, Keisha said, "Tutter, look momma has opened her eyes looking at you." I turned, got up, and took her hand. I told her to go on and rest. She was trying to tell me something but couldn't. I told her that God would let me know when the time was right, and she should just go on. She moved her head without assistance, smiled, looked up and said, "Ooooooooooooh, Oh My!!!!!" She saw something beautiful that made her extremely happy and went to her rest. Though we had that rough patch it never stopped my love for her. If we, more importantly, if I would have held on to who did what, then I would have missed such a wonderful emotional breathtaking moment—my mom's entrance into her resting place. This is how I choose to remember that moment because I was holding her hand while it was happening – sad and happy at the same time.

I was sitting alone on the porch late one evening, still wondering why I could not turn off the love for James. How can I love someone who has hurt me?? I didn't understand why he hurt me. I didn't understand what went wrong; my mind was all over the place in deep thought. I really needed answers that I didn't have and there was only one person who could give them to me. The one who I missed and loved, but yet I didn't want to see. I looked up and Sylvia (James' cousin and my long-time friend) was parking her car in front of my mom's house. I didn't know what she wanted but I was so glad to see her. She walked up saying, "Hey Hun, bless your heart, bless your heart" and then she hugged me. She sat on the porch next to me and asked how was I really feeling? I told her that she really didn't want to know. She said, "I can only imagine." I told her, "I'm confused. I'm hurt. I feel like a damn fool because I can't turn off my love for him. I'm wondering how is he doing. I can feel him somehow. I need to talk to him, but I am not ready. I am thinking about going home." I'm just in a confused place. She took me by the hand and said,

> Sweetie, I am not here to upset you, but James asked to come to see you. I came by two other times, but you were sleep so I told Claris Ann not to bother you. He wanted to know how you were doing. He wants you to know that he is sorry; he is so sorry. He needs for you to stop thinking, wondering what you did wrong because you did nothing wrong. It was him and his issues. He said that he was high, out of control because someone told him that you had a man in the house.

I turned to look at Sylvia with a shocking look because I had been wondering what happened. I was wondering when she pulled up and my thoughts were far from that. It wasn't even anything to think about because that was so far from the truth until it nearly took my breath away. I just could not wrap my brain around that one. All that I could say was, "Who in the hell would tell him some shit like that? What lowdown person hates me that much? Why would he believe that? All this time and this is why this happened??" I just sat there in disbelief crying, shaking my head. I just could not believe that a lie caused this hurricane to occur in my life, in our lives.

The conversation continued:

Sylvia: Sherry I also have some letters from him. He wanted to know if you were getting the ones that he mailed."

Me: Yes, but I just haven't opened them because letters weren't what I wanted.

Sylvia: I really didn't come to upset you, but he wanted to know if you still loved him.

I looked at Sylvia. I couldn't speak as tears were rolling down my cheeks. I started breathing hard; my mind was stuck between this lie, loving him still, wondering how he could believe such a thing. Who? Why? and how could somebody fix their mouth to tell him some shit like that knowing that he was a very jealous man and on drugs. I just looked at her, I really couldn't speak, my lips wouldn't move. I was so upset that my fingers were trembling. I was mad as hell. I was thinking if I saw him at that very moment, I would beat the hell out of him for even believing such a lie; but the reality was quickly setting in that he did believe it. I was hurt and hurting because he believed a lie! Sylvia hugged me and said, "LORD knows that I didn't come to upset you more than you already are. I am going to leave. If you want to talk, call me, baby. You got to believe how much that I hate that this has happened. I love the both of you. I am praying for the both of you; momma is too. Sherry what do you want me to tell him?" I just looked at Sylvia, I still couldn't speak. She touched me on my face, wiped my tears and told me that she will come back in a few days.

I sat on the porch for hours in the dark. I could not move and when I was able to speak, the only thing I yelled out was, "God Why? Why would somebody do this, say this? Did they want to hurt me personally and this was the only way that they could hurt me, the only way that they could see me hurt?" (Sometimes you think that you are completely healed from something, but you find out that you're not. As I am typing this, tears are rolling down my face. No, I am not angry. It's just that it hurt me so bad. The situation was extremely embarrassing to me. It was uncalled for. Maybe, hopefully this is the last time that I cry about this situation from my past. Prayerfully this is it, the final tears). I began to pray; I really was hoping that James was in his jail cell praying too because I refused to let a lie destroy me and my marriage. I just couldn't. I didn't know how I was going to go about fixing things, but what I did know, is that I needed the LORD. We needed the Lord and especially James needed the Lord because he was facing possible prison time.

Before I knew it, the sun was rising. I had been on the porch all night long thinking about how the devil and this person who lied to James couldn't win. I just kept thinking that the person would not get the end result that they were expecting. Somehow, someway we were going to get through this hurricane that purposely came to destroy us by using James' drug addiction to plant a seed to hurt me. I got up and yelled out:

> This is not the end! I don't care who thinks that I am stupid, crazy or whatever they think, it doesn't get to end this way! Whoever this is will get to see me and James better, so much better, closer than we ever been before. LORD my pop told me to pray and trust YOU and that's exactly what I am going to do. James will be the man that people aren't expecting him to be. Drugs will not end his story. This situation will not end our marriage. James Lynn Bobbitt made me a promise and he is going to keep it and I am going to keep mine. To death do us part, not some lie, not some lie, I refuse! With every fiber of my being, I simply refuse! Do you hear me Satan?! James Lynn Bobbitt doesn't belong to you. You can't mess with my mind concerning my marriage. I am going to get myself together so I can fight for my life, my marriage and my husband's life. I TRUST God that he will never see or be in prison over this matter. James will, he shall

> be the man that God wants him to be. Do I make myself clear? My God, MY God specializes in the things that seem impossible and this that I am BELIEVING God for is very much possible. People will get to see a marriage that appeared to be over, devasted, destroyed, demolished, wrecked, ruined and unheard-of surviving. Our marriage will override this ugly situation.

I went in the house and slept like a baby. I had not rested so peacefully in weeks. I woke up with a very different outlook on my current situation.

Later, that day Sylvia came by with a letter from James. I was in a better place, a better state of mind. We talked for a bit and she left. This time I opened a letter sent from him. It started out saying:

> I am so Thankful to God that you haven't stopped loving me. I know that you are mad at me and may be thinking about somebody from St. Louis or East St. Louis to come kill me. Please don't because you don't realize how sorry that I am that this happened. I wish that you would come and see me. I really need to see you and talk to you to explain myself. Sherry, Sugar Britches, Baby I promise you that this will never ever happen again. Last night at midnight I was hoping that you couldn't sleep, that you were praying because I was up praying. I was hoping and praying that we were asking God for the same thing—to fix our marriage—fix this situation for us to be better, so much better than we were. At times it felt like, to me, that you were praying while I was praying. Baby I know that you are hurt, hurting, mad, alone. I can only imagine the hell that Claris and Keisha are giving you because you aren't speaking negative about me. I know you, Sherry Evonne Jones Bobbitt. I know that your love for me didn't end because of this thing that should not

have happened. I should have never come home. I should have never listened and believed but I did. This is what I get for doing so. I hurt us: I almost lost us. The reason I sent Sylvia to ask you did you still love me is that I wanted to know what your eyes looked like. When she told me that you just looked at her crying, that your fingers were trembling, that you never said anything, that made me so happy. Sylvia thinks I am crazy, but I told her, she couldn't say, she wouldn't say what wasn't true. She hasn't stopped loving me. She is very mad, but the love is there, and I will spend the rest of my life with her loving me when I didn't deserve such a love in my life. Sherry people are going to talk, they are going to talk about us for a while and they are really going to talk about us when we get back together. I believe this with my heart and soul. When? I don't know but we will. I can't live without you, I just can't. I am messed up too and I messed up big time. I want to tell you what I prayed, what I prayed for you. Even if I have to serve time, I will keep praying this prayer because you are my wife, you will be my only wife. If you decide to leave me, I will still call you my wife but please give us a chance, please don't leave me. I have been reading a bible that a man gave me. He and some more people came to the jail to pray with us. He knew who I was from the newspaper; he knew who you were because you are one of his grandson's favorite teachers. He took me by my hands and said, 'Son have you really repented? Are you really sorry? Have you asked God to forgive you? Have you asked your wife to forgive you? Have you forgiven yourself?' I told him yes, I have asked God, I asked you in letters, but you wouldn't write me back. Then I told him that I didn't know that I had to forgive myself. He began to explain to me why I should.

He told me that you needed time, that I hurt you. What people were saying was hurtful and embarrassing and that I really needed to give you time—all of the time that you needed even if it took years because what you were dealing with was hard. Then he said, 'Son what if it were the other way around? What if you felt what she is feeling ten times worse? Give her time. She needs time to heal, and you can't heal her, it has to come from God.'

I prayed:

FATHER, please forgive me in the name of JESUS. I have hurt my wife so badly; I was hurting her and I couldn't seem to stop myself. It was like I was watching me hurt her and I didn't want to; I really didn't want to. I know that she needs time, plenty of time. She still loves me I know that she does. I can feel her love even though she is hurting. It is not wishful thinking. I can really feel her love. Please protect her heart. I know that people are making her feel bad because of what I did and what I have been doing. She is the one for me. I know that she will be with me until my dying day, and I almost lost her. Touch her in a special way that she does not feel crazy or foolish for still loving me. Let her feel that I am worth loving. Show me how to be and remain worth her love. She is so special, and I have been some kind of fool. Let her heart understand this fool and pray for me. Please let her keep praying for me. Nobody, nobody knows me better than she does but you. She calls me man of God and I keep getting high. What she sees in me, let me see it in myself. She is always praying for me. Sometimes she prays until she cries. She is a dreamer. Let her keep dreaming. LORD only you can help her out of this hurt. As I am praying, please let her be praying too. LORD have mercy, have mercy. I don't want to do time and she waste her life waiting on me because she will wait, and people will continue to hurt her. Touch her heart where she will feel like coming to see me. I can't do my part to fix this if she doesn't come to see me face to face. She has to look in my eyes and I must look into her eyes. When she looks in my eyes, please let her look in my heart. A better man is in me and if she sees that man, we have a chance. She always says that it's You, me and her and that's all that matters. Well one of us is hurting and LORD, you didn't do it I did! LORD, I don't know what her father is thinking but let him be better than Claris is being toward her. Please, please, please!

Sherry, there is more to the prayer but I don't have any more paper right now. Honey, I love you, I really love you and I know that I have done something that you may find hard to forgive me for but please forgive me. Even if you decide to leave me, please forgive me. Love always and forever your husband, James/Big Daddy. I miss you so much and I need you.

I read this letter over and over again. Somctimes seven times a day until finally I felt like seeing him. I was very nervous at the thought of seeing him, but I was ready. For some reason I didn't feel foolish with my present mindset. I was on a mission. I was in the fight of my life. As bad as things were, I couldn't give up. I didn't allow what people had to say about me, about him and about us to get in my way.

I knew that I dare not ask my mother or sister to take me. I didn't want a war or to hear their mouths. So, I fixed myself up for two reasons: (1) to make me feel better and, (2) to make this man realize that I was a very rare precious pearl that was in his hands to cherish and not throw away like trash. I just couldn't allow our relationship to end—not over this, not like this. It wasn't making sense to me. I felt it deep in my heart and I held onto the vision of my grandmother the night that James came home fighting me. She was there with me. She told me to be strong and let JESUS work it out. When I saw her, I thought that maybe it was my time, but she told me that it wasn't. She said, "Sometimes, you have to do things that seem nearly crazy but trusting God was all that I needed to do with my situation." She reassured me that I would be just fine. I was to hold my head up and remember what she told me before she had to leave. Remember her words and hold fast to what she said. For days I just focused on a conversation that took place when I was only seven years old but remembered it like it was just said to me.

I found it amazing when my mother asked me one day what I was thinking about, I told her what my Meemaw told me to remember. That's the night that James was fighting me, that she was with me. She told me that everything was going to be alright; that I had to trust God and remember what she told me.

My mother only looked at me. She didn't say a word. She took a deep breath and walked away. I often wondered did she remember that evening. Before my Meemaw passed away, she told my mom to bring me to her room and leave us alone. When she was finished talking to me, she told me to go get my mother. Together she told us, "The things that I have told my baby are for her. She won't have anybody's love and understanding when she most needs it. You won't understand. You will leave her out in the cold, and I need her to understand that I will be there for her in great times of need as the LORD allows me to. Do not question her, later or ever." My mother went for a walk. I was sitting on the porch when she got back. She said, "Do you want some ice cream?" I replied, "Yes, thank you." She brought it to me. We sat on the porch, ate ice cream and said nothing to each other. My mother didn't appear to be upset but you can tell that what I said weighed heavily on her mind.

While we were sitting there, Uncle Buck pulled up and told me that Daddy Boo (my grandfather) wanted to see me. Well, it wasn't like that I didn't know that he would send for me. I was very nervous but got up and went anyway. When I got there, he was sitting by the door in the den like he always did. I walked in and kissed him; he kissed me back. I sat down next to him in a chair at the kitchen table. No one was home so he was waiting for me alone. For a while he said nothing, then he said:

> "What did that Sum Bitch do that for?" I said, "I don't know. I am so confused. I just don't know." I started to cry and my grandfather said, "Hell, you gonna be alright Mrs. Sherry. Are you gonna stay with him? Because if you are, me and him got to talk first. I dreamed about Gin (my Meemaw)." He sat there with his legs crossed moving his fingers He rubbed his head, then said, "I thought that Sum Bitch had more since than that. He on them drugs I heard. I thought that he had it together better than that. Shit I just don't know about this but I dreamed about Gin. Well, you know bout what she said. Have you seen him yet?" I said, "No sir."

He said, "Well don't you need to at least find out what the hell happened? Cause you sure as hell ain't gonna find out until you do. I sure am disappointed in that boy." We just sat watching tv for a while, then he said, "I went and bought a watermelon and some peaches. Go on in the kitchen and cut us a piece of watermelon." This made me cry because watermelon and peaches were our thing. When I was a little girl, I would ride the Greyhound bus to Trenton. Back then Daddy Boo worked at a Texaco service station as a mechanic that was across the street from the bus station. He would always be there to pick me up. When I saw him, my world was smiling all over. When the door opened, he would speak to the driver and then say, "Is there a pretty little lady on this bus by the name of Miss Sherry?" The driver would say, "Why yes there is." Daddy Boo would be grinning from ear to ear, and I would be too. He would pick me up, hug and kiss me, get my luggage, take me by the hand and we walked across the street until it was time for him to go home for lunch. Meanwhile, he would buy me an RC Cola to sip on while I waited. The ride home would be fun because we stopped for a watermelon that I picked out and big bags of peaches for a peach cobbler. On the way home he would ask me to ask Meemaw to make us a peach cobbler. When we got to the house Meemaw would be in the kitchen acting like she didn't know that I was coming. I thought that she didn't. She would act so surprised.

I couldn't help thinking of those days while I was cutting up the watermelon. I felt like a little girl again. After we ate, he said, "Damn it, I don't like this shit and I don't know right directly what to do." He took me by my hand and said, "I don't care how old you get, you are still my baby, still my Miss Sherry. You hear me? You hear me?" I got up, sat on my granddaddy's lap and cried. He kept saying, "Go on and cry." I was missing my Meemaw and my aunt Yvonne so much, wishing that they were both still living. When I got ready to go home, he said, "When that boy gets out of jail, tell him I need to see him." I said, "What if he doesn't get out?" He said, "Gin told me to talk to him, he getting out." I hugged him and went back to my mother's.

Well, the moment was upon me. I was on my way to see my husband, not knowing what I was going to say, how I was going to react or if I would be able to even look at him. After walking to the jail, several times starting to turn around, I walked in. After signing in, the first thing I saw was his family. My heart started pounding. His mother wanted to know why I was there. I hadn't been there and why was I there now? Nobody spoke to me but his oldest brother, Lee, Jr. That brought me a little bit of comfort. He walked over to me and said what he always said, "Hey Sis. How are you doing?" He kissed me on the jaw and walked me over to where everyone was sitting. James's mom was still fussing. My sisters-in-law looked at me with frowns. Lee, Jr. said, "Let's go and let them talk." My mother-in-law wasn't feeling that. Lee, Jr. said, "Yes, we're all leaving! This man needs to explain to his wife why this shit happened! They need to sit down and talk alone!" He looked at James and said, "Brother I'll see you later. I hope that you all get this worked out." {Here I go crying again. I don't think that Lee, Jr. really knew how that made me feel that day. That gave me hope in what was seemingly like a hopeless situation despite me

TRUSTING God for my marriage. If Lee, Jr. has ever felt some kind a way about me, I have never heard it or felt it. You just don't know how good it felt to have at least one somebody in James family to feel this way and show it.} Lee, Jr. pulled the chair out for me to sit down and said, "Sis, I hope you all can work this out. I hope that you can forgive him." That brought me so much comfort.

Now it was just James and me. We only looked at each other and cried. He put his hand up against the glass. At first, I couldn't put my hand up, my heart was crushing in a different way with emotions in a place that they had never been before. After about five minutes, I thought he would move his hand, but he didn't. We kept crying and finally I put my hand up to touch the glass.

He said, "Did you feel that?" I said, "Yes." I started crying so hard because it felt like God had put HIS hands on OUR hands. (Wow, here I go with the tears again. I guess I will be doing this while completing this book.) We didn't say anything. I really don't think in that moment that it was anything for us to say. I felt that GOD was speaking, and we just had to listen in our spirits. We stayed that way until visiting hours were over. I had a relative working that night and he let me stay a little longer. The only thing that James said that night was, "I'm sorry. Please forgive me. This won't ever happen again, and I love you." After about ten minutes, I said, "I know, I have, it better DAMN not and I love you too. He then said, "Do you really still love me?" I said, "Yes, or else I wouldn't be here. I can't stop and you better get it together with a quickness because I can't go through this ever again. I mean never!"

It was time for him to go back to his cell. He should have already been back in. He asked if we could pray before I left. He prayed.

> LORD, thank you. Thank you so very much for seeing my wife safely here to see me. Please let this be the beginning of a new life together. Only YOU can turn things around so we can be together again. Please don't let my wife leave here regretting that she came and please

> don't let what people have to say bother her and continue to hurt her feelings. She has been hurt enough by people and me. Heal her as only you know how. Love on her in a special way and comfort her. Prepare her heart and mind to receive me. Let my touch not remind her of that ugly night but let her feel a brand-new touch from me—one that she will fall in love with. She loves being in love. Please don't let her stop! Please don't let her stop! I AM the man to be in her life. She didn't make a mistake by giving me her hand in marriage. I made the mistake. Hold her until you allow me to hold her again and YOU and only YOU will bring our marriage to an end. She is my wife for the rest of my life. AMEN! AMEN! AMEN!

I said, "AMEN! AMEN! AMEN!" with him. We kissed with glass between us. I really needed that.

The court date came. It was very embarrassing. Our mothers were there, my sister and plenty of people to see and hear what was going to happen. I was really feeling some kind a way because people were making sure that I could hear their remarks. I never turned around to see who was talking. Tony Johnson walked over to me and said,

> "Big Sister hold your head up. You are looking richer than Oprah today in this yellow dress. That nigga's heart is going to drop when he sees you. He already knows that he's gonna have to get his shit together. It's a few out here wanted to get next to you hoping that he does some time, but I hope that he gets out and you two make it. Don't let these unhappy people in here get you down. You handle your business and show them how it goes down when you let JESUS work it out."

Tony kissed me on my cheek and walked way. It's strange how I was looking for that to come from my mother, his mother, my sister that day but it came from Tony Johnson. Rest in peace Tony Johnson and again, Thank You!

I looked up and James's attorney was entering the room. He walked over to the table, sat his briefcase down, and turned around casing the room. He walked over to a young lady whose face was badly bruised. He introduced himself assuming that it was me and she immediately got upset and loud and said, "Naw naw I'm not her!" His attorney apologized walking back toward his seat I stood up when he got even with me. I said, "Excuse me, I am Mrs. James Lynn Bobbitt." He surprisingly looked at me as if he was amazed. He extended his hand and introduced himself to me. He told me he would be representing James and his job was to do what James and I had requested which was to make sure that James never see a day in prison and that we would be able to rekindle our marriage. I said thank you and took my seat and he returned to his.

After I sat down, I couldn't help but think that James's attorney was expecting me to look tore up from the floor up. But, to his surprise, by the grace of God, I was as radiant as radiant can be which caused him to probably think that my make-up was perfectly done to hide the bruises. The truth is I don't wear make-up like that, and I never did. It's amazing when you trust God and take him at his word that there is nothing impossible for him to do. Those bruises vanishing from my face overnight proved to me just how awesome, powerful, and amazing God is.

I stood up when James stood up. I was asked why I was there and what I wanted to say? I simply kept saying, "I was there for my marriage to have a chance to be redeemed." The crowd had all kinds of things to say. Finally, it was over. I got outside and my sister refused to give me a ride home, called me a stupid bitch and pulled off. I didn't have far to walk so I walked home, and I didn't feel bad. I felt happy! Our prayers were answered!! Til death do us part. Not a lie!

James spent only about two months in the Gibson County jail. When he got out, I picked him up, we went to Daddy Boo's. My granddaddy cussed him out royally telling him how disappointed he was and that he needed to be glad that I wanted to work things out because he wanted to kill him. James just listened and said, "Yes sir and that it would never happen again." Daddy Boo said, "Yeah, you make damn sure that it don't because the law won't be your worries son, it will be me. Understand me cause I ain't gonna say this no damn more. We won't have this talk again." I was surprised that James just sat there and took Daddy Boo's words and attitude without saying anything back. I asked James how did that make him feel? He said, "Sherry, he is your grandfather. He is hurt by what happened. You are his first grandbaby; he loves you and he was making sure that I understood where he was coming from. I was expecting for him to say more than what he did, he had every right to speak his mind."

We left town to spend a week together alone figuring out how to move forward. We spent a lot of time praying together and then we went home to find out we no longer had a home. Our landlord told us that we had two weeks to move. Another hurdle to jump but we made it.

In order to tell our truth throughout this chapter I mentioned things that some may not have wanted to be included, and I can understand that. However, if I write this any other way, there are others who also know the truth. I hold no grudges against anyone who wasn't there for me during our hurricane season. Despite your absence, you had a key role in that season. You caused me to cling closer to God's comfort, to trust him and BELIEVE him for a miracle that ONLY he could manifest! James and I walked away from that season with a stronger prayer life together. Our marriage survived. We were able to teach other married couples. I could go on with the great number of things that were birthed from our hurricane season. Because of not having the love and support that I thought I needed, the action from those who, what I considered, abandoned me actually did me a tremendous favor pushing me into the ARMS OF OUR GOD—the very best place for me. I got to keep my marriage/our marriage. My husband became the man of God that he was supposed to be.

James has left a legacy and mine is yet to come. I truly wish that everything could have been done differently. I even wish that the lie was never told which caused many to have different feelings during that season. This I consider indeed my all things working together. Yes,

Romans 8:28, "And we know that all things work together for the good of them that love God, to them who are the called according to his purpose." Yes! Romans 8:28 doing what it does. To God be the GLORY!!!!!!! Like a cake, you can tolerate a spoon full of sugar better than you can a spoon full of flour. You can't possibly make a good cake without both. So, it really doesn't matter to me if your role during our hurricane season was sugar or flour, I needed both. James and I needed both!

Time went by and we moved to Nashville, Tennessee. There were many golden opportunities for both of us. Moving was the best thing for us. Life was better…so much better. James gave his life to Christ, and we were baptized together. Life was moving on another level.

We always felt the need to be transparent about our marriage because you never know what may happen…and they did begin.

I was invited to speak with a panel of women concerning marriage relationships. We were all given a specific topic. Mine was "The Joys of Romance." I was excited because this is one of my favorite topics when it comes to marriage. I did as requested and it went extremely well. Afterwards, lunch was served. During this time, I went into the ladies' room. While in the stall, I overhead a conversation about me…a conversation about our hurricane season. I could not make out the voices. I didn't know anyone there except the minister who invited me. I was frozen. It felt as if Holy Spirit covered my mouth and bridled my tongue. I was extremely happy that lunch was the conclusion of the event. After they left, I could only laugh in spite of being hurt because it was opposite of what the conference was about.

I freshened up and went back into the fellowship hall. I was hoping to hear those voices to ask them why they didn't ask me about the situation. I certainly would have told them the truth and given them some clarity. I felt like there would be a chance to do so, but this wasn't the time or place.

When I got home, James was sitting on the porch with our dog. As soon as I pulled up, he stood up ready to greet me. I got out of the car, he said, "Sugar Britches what's wrong? I feel like something is wrong. Baby come talk to me." I walked up to him, and he just held me for a while.

Then I told him what happened. He asked me how I wanted to handle the situation because it seems as if there were people in Nashville who wanted me crushed before I could make friends. I shared with him the experience that I had been unable to speak and heard "not now". He said, "What have you been saying? We must stay transparent with this because the devil has some people that are ready to embarrass you anywhere and embarrass us. We went in the house and, after helping me undress, James prayed for me.

> LORD, YOU gave my wife the gift of being an awesome speaker. It took SOOO long for her to see and accept this gift. Now she is here. There are people waiting to knock her down before she can get in the door. LORD, PLEASE!! PLEASE give her the strength to hold her head up, walk in a room knowing that the enemy has a trick up his sleeve, do what YOU sent her to do without sounding offended, but certainly making a statement. Let her conduct and character speak through the noise. I wish that I could go back in time and take that ugly season away because I am to blame. No matter who said what and why, I am to blame. If I wasn't on drugs, it wouldn't have happened.
>
> LORD, PLEASE pour into my wife what she needs to stand in the faces of those who want to remember the dark parts of our life when she is standing in the light on a platform. Let her use that as a teaching tool. Let her stand boldly speaking truth in such a transparent way until it makes the people talking wish that they would have kept their mouths closed. My wife is a class act. She is Mrs. One-of-a-kind. You designed her for this so please shield her heart. Put a hedge of protection all around her as she treads over everything being said. I know that this caught her by surprise. Let her not get caught up in finding out

who is saying what, but take what they are saying to say 'But look at what the LORD has done' in my life. Let her be able to say with joy in her heart, 'what the enemy meant for bad, God turned it around for my good.' LORD, she is a force to be reckoned with. YOU created her. You made her for this walk, for this journey. Raise her up before those who thought that our hurricane season was going to break her down and keep her bound in shame. She has nothing to be ashamed of. Only you can pour into her what is needed for a time and season such as this. There is a great calling on her life. I almost helped the enemy destroy that. Let not another do so. I ask that you give me insight where I may see trouble standing near so she can stay focused. This is YOUR daughter. Have YOUR WAY LORD!! HAVE YOUR WAY!! As she sleeps tonight, take out and put in. Let her wake up with a different outlook. LORD, I got the feeling that I might not even be ready for the next stage. So, while YOU are working on my wife, please PLEASE work on me because we are a team. I pray this prayer in the name of JESUS CHRIST. AMEN! AMEN! AMEN!

Well, a next time came, and they kept coming. Finally, there was the chance to be in a conversation with Pastor Michael Cousin and His wife, Minister Freda Cousin. James and I shared with them "us" because there were things asked of us in his ministry. We were very transparent with them before spending a season in their ministry One reason was there were people who attended the church who knew about that part of our lives. Wow! It happened but not until I was asked to speak. We never heard anything as long as James was doing something. When the bones were being dug up and brought to the Pastor and First Lady's attention, they simply said that they already knew. If you know Freda Cousin, she looked over her glasses (as she always does) and said, "Is that what you wanted to talk to us about?" She would then ask, "What was the REAL reason for wanting them to know."

I often think of that prayer and smile because having a praying husband is like having a semi-automatic weapon that you don't have to use because the power of prayer is so much greater. After all these years it still happens, and I find it so tired and old.

WOW! As I have come to a close of this chapter, Anthony Hamilton's song, *Can't Let Go* is playing on the radio. This song wasn't out during our hurricane season, but it was one of our favorites. It is strange how things happen. I have been crying throughout this chapter and to have that song play summarizes what I have explained about us during this season. It was a season that came with many teachable moments, life changing experiences, and not being able to let go!!

Those types of storms are ones that the enemy, and a few folks, thought would surely take them out and destroy her life. All I can say is, "BUT GOD!!!!!" We did NOT let go until we had no other choice! I would never encourage anyone to take the journey that was ours only, but what I hope is there are nuggets in this chapter that will help someone to seek God together for ALL matters in their marriage relationship and make sure that it is HIM that is leading and guiding you both through your journey together.

Truth is, I have yet to know exactly why God ORDAINED us to stay together. For some reason, I truly trusted HIM to get us through the journey. As a matter of fact, that is a prayer that James never prayed with me. This is truly one to be chalked up as ONLY God KNOWS!

Before I end this chapter, let me say that my little sister apologized to me as well. She told me that she has always known how much James and I loved each other, in spite of the hurricane season, but when he left, she missed the "us." She regrets that his absence has given her a greater understanding of what God's purpose was. She, her children and grandchildren have heard me talk and cry to James in my sleep as if he was still here. She now prays for me and blesses me with text messages when she feels my pain. I am blessed to have nieces that do the same.

~POEM~

Like two palm trees in the midst of a hurricane season,
We only lost a few branches but held tightly to each other for many good reasons.

Truly a season in our marriage that we wished had never happened, but it had.
We never pretend that it didn't, I do believe that a few people and the Devil were the only one's mad!

This hurricane season brought forth many unexpected blessings for us.
One was we had to move from saying and start to live in the God we TRUST!

We learned how to always talk to each other, getting an understanding between us before allowing anyone to interfere.
Most of all to keep God in the midst and to keep loving even when our hearts felt fear.

We didn't have a perfect marriage, nor was it trouble free.
Our bond was that I loved James and James loved me.

Many people couldn't believe how transparent we were in our marriage with no shame.
The wounds of the past, the pains that they brought, the tears that had fallen didn't dictate who we were, so the past wasn't able to manifest itself to remove us from the loving, Godly couple that we became.

We knew that one of us, if not both, would one day be in the limelight.
Once you get there, people love to bring up your past,
So that's why we chose to live shameless, so the conversations would hold no weight and therefore they wouldn't last.

It certainly happened a time or two,
Each time an ugly whisperer had gossip to spread, who they told already knew.

We learned quickly how to stay one step ahead of the enemy's traps and snares.

People didn't know just how much and how many times together we prayed to a God WHO CARES.

So, this made it easy for us to live in love together.
Leaving many wondering how are they still with each other after the most horrific type of weather.

The hurricane was meant to destroy our love and peace, designed to bring our marriage to an end.
Committed to our vows made it hard to walk away from the relationship of lover and friend.

Some may call us crazy, join the club many have said the same,
We came together in prayer because neither of us wanted to change my last name.

Together in love with love until his dying day,
Now, holding him in a chamber of my heart when alone I pray.

Author: Sherry E. (Jones) Bobbitt
My Song Choices: *There's No Me Without You* by The Manhattans
Finding My Way Back by Jaheim

CHAPTER 10: THE PRAYER FOR COURAGE TO RETURN TO CHURCH

Let's just keep it 1000! Sometimes church folk make you more uncomfortable than the people in the world. It was months before we returned to church together, which left my tummy in knots just to think about it. I went only once while James was locked up and it was very uncomfortable with people talking about me where I could hear them. I thought that going to church would make me feel better, but I walked home in tears and vowed to never treat anyone the way that I was treated. I almost considered never going back to church. I really do understand how people can feel this way concerning church hurt.

One Sunday morning James said, "Honey, you know that we are going to have to eventually go back to church." I said, "Yes, I know but you don't know how I felt. I never thought that there was such a feeling to have. I was already nervous and embarrassed, but I was not expecting, in a million years, the reception that I got. I really didn't know what was going to happen, but I would never cause anybody to feel the way that I was feeling." James said, "But we can't let them and what happened keep us out of church." I agreed that the following Sunday would be the Sunday. When that day came, he had to pull the car over so I could throw up. We went back home and then it was diarrhea. My nerves were shot. James finally understood just how I was affected by my first visitation. Later that day, he woke me up to see if I was ready to drink some ginger ale and eat some crackers. We sat talking about how to get passed our feelings and go back to church. He reminded me that this time we would be together. That was enough for me. Later that week James saw my cousin, Juanita Smith. She told him that she missed seeing us in church. He told her why we weren't coming. When he told me that he saw her and about the conversation, I was pissed off. The next thing I knew she was knocking at the door. I listened to her, and it did not help me. I did enjoy her coming to see me because she was always a very sweet person.

After bible study that Wednesday evening, our Pastor, Rev. Clifford Martin, stopped by. I absolutely did not want to talk but James let him in. After I entered the room, James and I started the conversation by apologizing for our wrong doings. We used the church phone for us to talk to each other which ended up costing a lot. I thought that when the church received the phone bill that it would be brought to my attention, and I could explain and take care of it. It did not turn out that way. The biggest part of the problem was that we didn't ask for permission. Rev. Martin explained that the matter was taken care of, and we shouldn't allow that to keep us out of church. We let him know that after my experience, I wasn't ready to go back until I felt stronger. Rev. Martin then apologized to us saying, "He wasn't there for us like he should have been. He felt bad about not coming by to see me when he knew that my feelings were hurt when I came to church. Some people made it even worse, and he said nothing." The three of us ended up in tears and Rev. Martin prayed. Before he left, he wanted us to know that he hoped to see us on that Sunday but if not then, very soon.

Two more Sundays had gone by, and I still wasn't ready. James said, "Sherry, please let me pray for you. Honey, you have too much to offer. You are too gifted to be out of church this long. You can't let what people say or do keep you away." I agreed and he prayed.

His prayer was:

> LORD, we come right now in the mighty name of JESUS! LORD my wife needs a touch from you. She needs to hear from you. I have done all that I can do to encourage her. I don't know how she is really feeling because I haven't gone to church yet, so please take this feeling, these feelings away from her. Please give her the joy back. Shield her from all of the noise, LORD. Please don't let her hear the noise. YOU know what she needs to get over this, get through this better than I do, so I am

> depending on YOU to help us. Help my wife. Let something happen to ease her fear and pain. FATHER, please forgive me. This is all my fault. If I didn't make this huge mistake, she wouldn't be on this emotional roller coaster right now. LORD, we need to be in church this Sunday. Wrap YOUR ARMS around my wife as I wrap my arms around my wife. LORD, please go before us and clear the way. I ask this of YOU LORD in the PRECIOUS NAME OF JESUS!!! AMEN! AMEN! AMEN!

For the first time I didn't say AMEN with James. I wanted to but I didn't. I was just in a place. I really wanted to attend a different church, but we went to Martin Tabernacle anyway. It took me at least ten minutes to get out of the car. We walked in. People were looking at us, some tapping others on the shoulder. Only one person looked at us and smiled. It was Aunt Lucille, Ray and Sylvia's mom. I was still very uncomfortable for so many reasons. Church seemed to be a little late getting started that Sunday which made it worse to me. James was also uncomfortable. We sat as close to each other as we could holding hands. I was so upset that I could have burst into tears. In comes Monica Herron, fashionably late as always. She walked in, took her seat, then looked over at James and me. All of a sudden, she stood up, started clapping her hands very loudly, yelling, "Thank You LORD, PRAISE THE LORD!!" She kept saying it over and over again clapping her hands. She continued as she walked to the back of the church. People were looking at her like what's going on with Monica. She walked over and stood behind James and me putting her arms around us. Crying she said,

I am so glad to see you both in church this morning. I am so glad to see that you are still together. I love the both of you. I always have, I always will. You will get through this. You all will make it when other marriages will fail for a lot less. God has a plan and a reason for you two to stay together. Don't let what nobody has to say separate you two. Let the LORD handle this!

She kissed both of us and walked back to her seat yelling, "Look what the LORD has done, look what the LORD is doing!!

That—right there—was what I needed, what James and I needed. It came from someone that we weren't expecting to react in such a way, but it was truly what we needed. All I could think about was that was God in Monica, God using Monica Herron to let us know that HE was with us, that James and I were not alone. Romans 8:31 came to James's mind. He whispered to me, "If God be for us, who can be against us?" This was starting to feel better. I actually felt like being in church after all. Over the years I have told Monica how that sincerely blessed me and that I will never forget that Sunday. I asked her, like I have asked others, can I share what they said in this book. She was delighted. James and I talked about that Sunday a few days before he passed away. We had joyful tears together as we were thanking God for our journey so far.

After church that Sunday we went to James Uncle Thelma and Aunt Maggie's home. They were glad to see us, to see us together and to know that we went to church. We had dinner with them. After dinner Uncle Thelma had a long talk with us. He told James that he needed to talk to him alone and they went outside. I helped Aunt Maggie clean the kitchen. After a while she asked me to sit. She shared with me the FAITH in God that I needed from that point until God sees fit to take one of us on. She shared the importance of truly forgiving and not letting what others had to say to cause me to go back on my word. She shared how she regretted that it took place, how she and Uncle Thelma cried and prayed together concerning us. She also shared how they missed us coming to visit them, taking them for rides and just coming to sit a spell. She hugged me and cried. While holding me she said, "Baby, I know that this has been so hard on you because you never stopped loving that boy. I know that you didn't because you couldn't. I know that you just couldn't and no, you ain't crazy, just keep on TRUSTING God only. Only God will see you through this and HE will make it like it never happened. There will be folks that will like to remind you about it, but you never mind them and let them talk.

I can't say what Uncle Thelma talked to James about. All I know is they came in the house with tears and Aunt Maggie and I were the same. James never asked me what we talked about, and I never asked him what they talked about. We were just blessed to have them talking to us. On our way home, we didn't say anything, just held hands. He got to the by-pass and started driving toward Jackson. We went for ice cream and cried. On the way back home to Trenton he said, "I hope that you really understand how sorry that I am, and I hope that you stay strong because we are still going to have a wonderful life together." I said, "I know. I have and yes, we will. I will be holding your hand until the very end, the end that God Has planned.

From time-to-time James and I would talk about that visit with Uncle Thelma and Aunt Maggie and how it was a wonderful day for a day starting out with fear of what was going to happen.

There is nothing like wisdom talking TO you and not AT you!

I would be remiss to not mention the special hugs from two of our church babies, Rachel Penn and Choya Manierre. They were in tears. I was positive that they had been around adults talking and really didn't know what to say, so they cried. I knew that they were glad to see us and just didn't know how to express themselves, but we felt the love.

I'm sure many others may have felt the same because during times such as this, people were saying so much that wasn't true. Naturally people were taking sides and, the sad part was, that nobody took us aside. Because of our experience, we made a vow to be the "go to" couple when trouble came in marriages that we knew. Not just to be one's that they could talk to but one's that they could confide in. It was so very important to James and me to help couples in trouble. We never shared it with others as we considered it a private ministry that God ORDAINED for us.

~POEM~

Desire left my heart to walk back through the church door,
Deeply wounded on so many levels with my head hung while my tears hit the floor.

Thinking that this was always the place to run to for comfort and peace,
Unexpectedly bounded more, my pain impassable with no ability to release.

A part of me longing for Worship and Praise that I had missed so much,
Trampled by ugly vibes with a cold reception, unable to feel The MASTER'S TOUCH.

Being a babe in CHRIST I didn't know that Worship and Praise could be done alone anywhere,
I was accustomed to being in the midst of church family. Enjoying time spent with God was a time on Sundays to share.

Waiting on my husband to return home thinking that this feeling would go away,
Meanwhile I was smitten by a very strong pulling in my spirit that I shouldn't go astray.

To my surprise, My King, my husband was feeling somewhat the same,
Guilt was his issue because he played a part in our hurricane season that brought us much shame.

We weren't ready. I had the bad experience, he hadn't yet,
I could only share how going to church alone was something that I did regret.

I knew that people would whisper and stare,
But an unwelcome, unkind atmosphere just wasn't fair.

We were encouraged to return to church. I just couldn't stand to have that experience again.
Going alone was truly a huge mistake for me, left feeling like I had not one friend.

We returned. He was experiencing a shunning that he never had,

I really was hoping with us being together for the return not to be so sad.

Sitting in the back of the church third from the last pew, holding hands in a cloudy room very close together,
Suddenly God sent Monica in as if she were JESUS to shift the weather.

Truly, her actions were like a blanket of love that brought such warmth to us,
Our focus quickly turned back to THE ONE that we trust.

Church hurt is a real feeling. It comes with so much harm to those who are struggling to come in from their storm and rain,
Love and compassion should be ready to embrace, inject comfort and kind words instead of an abundance of more pain.

A lesson learned on how to guard our hearts/ heart because even within the church some may bask in your downfall,
From that experience, we stop waiting to get to church for an altar call.

Author: Sherry E. (Jones) Bobbitt
My Song Choices: *Open My Heart* by Yolanda Adams
Like A Dew by Juanita Bynum

CHAPTER 11: THE PRAYER FOR MY GIFT OF WRITING

Everybody in my family could sing but me although I did ok at times. My thing was writing. I love poetry and creative writing. My pop used to get mad at me for using up so much notebook paper. For some reason, I kept it a secret because I didn't know anybody that loved poetry and I didn't want to be teased for being different. As I grew older, I wrote more. I had an allowance then, so I could buy my own paper.

My mom told me that she had to always pop my hands for scribbling on everything, even when I couldn't put words together. I could properly hold a pencil and ink pen by age one. One day she spanked my hands at the doctor's office for scribbling on the magazines. She said that an elderly white lady told her to stop spanking me. Mom said she explained to the lady that I wrote on everything jabbering and she was trying to teach me not to. Well, this lady told mom that she was a retired schoolteacher and that she was finding joy watching me scribble, jabber and hold an ink pen better than some adults. I was nearly two at the time. She went on to tell mom that I had a gift in writing that was being developed and one day, if mom would stop spanking and encourage me, she was sure that, one day, I would become a wonderful writer. Mom said the lady told her not to destroy my gift. So many parents destroy their children's gifts because they don't recognize it as a gift. She also told mom to introduce me to paper; give me my own box with paper, pencils and crayons. She was to then help me understand that I am to only use what was in my little box. Well for mom at the time, it went in one ear and out of the other. I was a very good listener until it came to scribbling and jabbering in a whisper. One day we were in my mom's hometown in Trenton, TN. There I was at it again. My mom started to spank me but my granddaddy, Daddy Boo, told her to leave me alone. He seemed to enjoy watching me so busy and so serious. He called my Meemaw in the room and mom said that they just watched me. Then I walked over to Daddy Boo, showed him my paper and started jabbering. He looked at my Meemaw and said, "Shit, she is saying something; we just don't know what it is yet." Mom said that Meemaw said, "Nobody made you stop jabbering and finally your jabbering turned into singing. Our baby is going to be a writer. She's going to write something special one day." Mom said that she went outside because they had spoken and that was it. So, she got the little box together for me. There I was at two beginning my writing career that for many years I kept a secret. I was able to keep this a secret until high school. Being kind of shy, I really kept my gift hidden, even from my closet childhood friend, Mrs. Kathy Ford Payne.

Once a guy who was a senior in high school started calling me notebook girl. I was a sophomore, but we had a class together. He would ask what I was always writing. I never answered him. One day he snatched my notebook just as we were changing classes and read my poem. I stood there with tears rolling down my cheeks. He said, "Damn notebook girl. Why are you crying? This is deep, this is really deep. Oh man, I know who this is about." I asked him not to do that to me. Please don't say anything. He gave my notebook back to me and said, "Damn stop crying. Don't trip. I'm not gonna say nothing to"...(whispering in my ear who it was). He kept his word, and I was so relieved. Again, I had a secret until a classroom assignment in Mrs. Paulette Kirkwood's class. We had to have a partner for the assignment. I didn't want to speak so I wrote. My partner did not do a very good job. I was very disappointed in the presentation and the grade that we received. Mrs. Kirkwood pulled me aside and told me the written work was beautiful, but I should have gotten up and spoke. She sort of let me have it. She ended the conversation with:

> If you are going to be a writer of poetry, you're going to have to start opening up your own mouth. If I can't hear you speak from your soul, then how can I begin to understand what you are feeling and what you meant and feel the passion that you are writing in? Your mouth,

> you can speak. You have a gift, Miss Jones. Until you realize it, nobody will truly understand your passion for writing. Bring the words off the paper. Let them flow from your heart through your mouth Miss Jones.

Man, she was very firm with me that day. I almost cried. I know that my eyes were full of tears but that didn't seem to move her. For that she came off my Cool Teacher's list.

Many years went by and now I was with James, the man that I loved, but did not share my passion for writing with him. After nights of heated moments, deep passion, chandelier experiences, James would always sing, or music would be playing…just him expressing how he was feeling. I would wait for private moments to write poems about how he made me feel. He would often question how I felt because I never deeply expressed myself like he did. I did express myself, but only on paper. Why??? Because I was accustomed to keeping all of my writings private. I felt these were my private feelings…not even to be shared with him.

One day when I came home from shopping, there he was with one of my notebooks—the one that was all about him. I was very upset. I started crying, yelling that he had no rights to my personal belongings. He looked at me and said:

> Why are you tripping with me? Why don't you tell me these things? Why are you crying and why do you hide this? Honey, this is beautiful. Hell, this is deep. Don't you know that you should be able to share this with me? Why don't you feel free to read these poems to me? Who hurt you where you feel ashamed of this? Damn girl this is off the chain. You got me all hard just reading this. Look! Look at me! My boy stiff as a board. You turn me on but damn this right here, I need you to sit down and read it to me. I need to hear this in your voice and calm down.

He poured himself some Crown, me a glass of wine, and rolled us a joint. After we started drinking and smoking, he said, "I need you to relax, just relax and read to me. Please read to me and start with the front where my name is." It took me a few minutes and another joint before I began. It was the look in his eyes from that moment that gave me the courage to read to him some of the poems that were about him and the ways that he made me feel. I was truly set free that night from the bonds of shame. Well, I really don't have to go into details of how that night ended, ok! A few days later I was in the kitchen washing dishes and he called me into the bedroom. He was sitting on the bed with a very serious look on his face. He said, "Sherry Jones, we need to talk…talk about your poems, your writings and why you hide this. Better yet, let me just pray for you because I don't want to say the wrong thing.

I started dropping tears, closed my eyes and said, "Ok, James." He prayed:

> LORD, I really don't know where to start because I don't want to offend my baby. She has such a beautiful gift and I know that it had to come from YOU. Please, show me how to help her with her gift. I don't know much about poetry, but I feel that she is really good at this. I'm so proud of her. So many hidden talents from the diamond in the rough and she is not seeing what I see and hear. She said that she was free, but I just wanted her to be absolutely sure that she is free. I shouldn't be the only one hearing this. LORD, she's deep, I mean really deep, and she has to understand that it's time to share this with others because it is worth sharing. Whatever has been planted in her to keep this to herself, uproot it please, destroy it. Whoever made her feel bad about this, whoever didn't see it as a gift, let her not hold on to those things but let YOU work this out of her so she can share this

> special gift with the world. LORD, I know that there will be people who will feel the way that I do about her gift. Please don't let her die with this gift and somebody else gets the credit for her skills because she has skills. I am asking for this very special blessing in the mighty powerful name of JESUS!! AMEN! AMEN! AMEN!

We laid down and took a nap after that prayer. I woke up to finish the dishes, but he had finished them. When I walked into the living room, he had scented candles lit, soft jazz playing, wine poured, joints rolled, laying on a blanket in front of the sofa. He said, "Did you enjoy your nap? I started to wake you up so we can go somewhere but I thought that this would be better. Come join me and see where we go from here." No sex, just passion and intimacy and it was topped off with the sun kissing our faces the next morning.

As, time went by, through a conversation with James while putting up some ceiling fans for my cousin Juanita Smith, she asked me to write a play for the young adults to do at church. Naturally, I was reluctant to do it, but since I was set up, I did it anyway.

I can't recall what the play was about. I feel ashamed because my heart was not in it. I only remember that James, Monica Avery Harris, Terri Bolden, Charmaine Washington and a few others were in it. We were the young adults during that time, and it was received well.

From there, I was writing Easter speeches, small skits and plays. I began rendering occasions at different church and non-church functions. James said, "A star was born." Naturally, you always have your critics and James wasn't letting that stop me, he wasn't having it.

In 1993 a lady named Cynthia asked me to write a skit for the Brownsville-Dyersburg District Christmas program which I did because Valerie Mack, the Usher President insisted. It went over better than I expected. In 1994 Ms. Rose Mitchell asked me to think about being in the annual conference young adult pageant. This was beginning to be too much for me. I was feeling like I had gotten into something that I couldn't get out of. Then cousin Juanita asked me (why I could never say no to her, I don't know). I wrote a skit, not knowing what the pageant was about. The day came and it was show time. I made my costume. The skit was called *A Slave Girl's Dream.* I portrayed two people—something I had never done before. It was at Mother Liberty Church in Jackson, Tennessee. We had never been there before. When James pulled up, my heart dropped. This was a Cathedral – not the small churches that I was used to being in. When we walked in, it looked like there were over 500 people. My nerves were shot! James said, "Girl, look at all of these people. It's your time, this is your awaiting audience. Honey this is it! This is the moment that I have been waiting for." Before I could comment, I was asked to go to a room where the other pageant contestants were. There were at least 20 young women back there none of whom I knew. They were busy dressing doing their own thing. Cousin Juanita came to see if I needed help getting dressed. She was grinning from ear to ear, and I wanted to run. Finally, we were all dressed. We went out to sit off to the side. As they were getting up with their many different talents, I felt like I didn't have a chance. Finally, it was my turn. It was such a blur for me. I had to remove myself mentally in order to perform. We all had to exit down the center aisle and it was a long one.

When I finished, I could not believe the response. The audience was on their feet, clapping, some had tears rolling down their cheeks. The entire time that I was walking down the aisle, people were clapping and standing up. To top everything off, there was my husband standing waiting for me, clapping with tears rolling down his cheeks. He greeted me with a hug, kiss and some lilies. (I love lilies.) I left the sanctuary to get out of costume. I went outside, walked around to the front entrance and sat with James. He wanted to know why I didn't sit with the other contestants. I said, "I'm sure that I didn't place, so we can just leave afterwards. It came time for the judging of the talent competition. I did not do anything for the Queen part, so I would be ready to go after the talent section. The 4th, 3rd and 2nd place winners were announced. By now I was ready to go not expecting to win.

We stood up to leave and they said my name. I was frozen and James was yelling, "I knew it! I knew it! Go get your trophy girl. You won, Baby you won!"

Finally, I believed that I had talent. I had a gift.

James always believed in me when I didn't believe in myself. He was my cheerleader, my booster, my encourager! He experienced something with me that my own parents had never experienced with me. He was my first on so many levels in my life.

~POEM~

My man believed in my gifts before I knew they were so,
His love moved me from a place of shame to freely letting go.

For so many years my love of poetry and creative writing was kept deep within,
Fear of being ostracized, I never shared my gift with anybody, not even my closet friend.

I was rushed into adult like responsibilities at such an early age,
Poetry became my way to talk about how unfair life was at times, dramatically casting roles, center stage.

Many times, when I wanted to cry writing dried my tears,
Pen and paper have kept my most intimate secrets down through the years.

Sitting alone for hours with so many dramatic views flowing from my heart and mind,
Trying hard to reach that silver lining that was getting harder and harder to find.

Often yelled at because I could get easily lost in time and space,
Unable to hear my mother's voice until she was standing directly in front of my face.

I never charged her because of my ability to drift away and lose track of time,
Only wishing that she would once ask me why, finding her lack of interest was a bit of a crime.

Finding it so hard to let James into this part of my life fearing that he might not care,
So, I continued with my time alone writing about the love we loved to share.

It wasn't until I felt that he broke into a part of my world when he wasn't invited to be there,
With tears after spending much time reading my work, he felt it was wrong of me not to share.

Having someone to find joy and admiration in my love of poetry was new to me,
My husband strongly expressing that it was a joy for us that had to be.

Words from my heart, placed on paper tucked away,
Once written to never see the light of day.

Gently pulled into the sunshine from the darkness of shade,
I began to share all that I had written about him from the love we had made.

Being so used to sailing alone with only my thoughts, paper and pen,
I invited James to my Island of Paradise and continued to write about our love—a love that I never wanted to end.

Author: Sherry E. (Jones) Bobbitt
My Song Choices: *Forever More* by Anthony David
featuring Algebra and Phonte
On The Ocean by K'Jon

CHAPTER 12: THE PRAYER FOR MY HEART, PASSION, DEEP LOVE AND DESIRE FOR ROMANCE

One weekend I was really feeling "All Extra"...I mean just still on that cloud that James laid me down on the night before. He had several service calls (he was an electrician) that Saturday which left me enough alone time to do me because my frame of mind just wasn't capable of doing anything else. I was absolutely engulfed in my "paradise of love land" thoughts.

I completed my desire for the evening which I already knew that, even after all of these years, it still caught him by surprise and caused tears of joy. When James opened the door, he just said, "My girl! My girl!" His tears began to flow! He said, "Let me freshen up. Don't move because I won't be long" and he wasn't.

He sat down beside me, kissed the "marriage hand" and said, "I got to pray."

He prayed:

FATHER! FATHER! I JUST WANT TO THANK YOU!!!!! What did I do to deserve such a wonderful loving wife! LORD, I do not take for granted that she has to do what she does because men have dreams and thoughts too. This woman, YOUR daughter, my wife is so full of the sweetest thoughts of romance. LORD, this is why I get so jealous. I just don't want her to ever be this good to another man and I know it because of her desire to always touch my heart, even when it's unworthy of such love like this. Bless her heart to never stop seeing marriage as she sees it. Please let her passion move to a level that is deeper than where she is so one day she will write 'love poetry' that is stimulated by the love that we have and share together. LORD! Her deep love and desire for romance is a 'mini series' in my life and happy is this man to have and hold a woman such as this. Please!! Please!!, not as long as I am living, let her only do these things for me and me alone. Keep her in a place where she always sees things in colors bold and bright as she says. LORD I really do appreciate what we have. I just want her to hear me say to YOU just how blessed that I am. By chance, if I go first, please let her keep this type of love alive because it's not just in the movies...it's real, it's real!! IN JESUS' WONDERFUL NAME I ask this of YOU, praying this prayer by faith IN JESUS' NAME. AMEN! AMEN! AMEN!

Now let me share one of the many different moments that brought his heart to, once again, pray like he did.

While James was away, my mind went into my place of "romantic bliss!" So, I went to the store to get everything that I needed to make it another night that he would not ever forget. Plus, knowing that he had never had the experience before made it even more special.

When he opened the door, he was truly knocked off his feet, especially after asking me what I wanted to do that day and my only response was "an evening just chillin with you." There I was, in a red dress, sitting on a red and white quilt. I also had red bulbs in the lamps, white candles lit, a sheer piece of fabric hanging from the ceiling like a canopy with clear Christmas lights on top of it. Additionally, I had a folding table with the legs still folded with a white lace tablecloth with some red fabric underneath. On it was champagne in a bucket, two champagne glasses, two shot glasses, a bottle of crown, a small meat tray, fruit and cheese tray, a vase with red roses and white carnations (his favorites) and soft music playing. I simply said, "Honey, let's chill." Oh my, oh my we did...and I mean we did.

THE PRAYERS THAT HE PRAYED FOR ME

~POEM~

Thoughts being birthed from the love that was made,
Filling my desire to take us on another paradise escapade.

Oh James had his own level of surprise romantic flow,
We were always willing to go as far as love would allow us to go.

Swimming deeply into a passion blinded by its light,
We being always together made it simple and right.

Sensations bursting and beaming from our toes,
While we are glued together nose to nose.

Glancing in the eyes of the other's love,
Patiently and yet intensely panting for the moment that the hand fits perfectly into the glove.

Memories made, photos taken with the minds and showers of love saturated the heart to a loving bliss,
Sealing together another breath-taking journey to "our love island" with a long passionate kiss.

Unable to speak leaving our voices all in our touch,
With a silent scream in harmony we're both saying "I Love You So Much!"

Together placing another romantic moment that was written in stone,
Where we could truly go to the places of the "sexy and grown."

This intimate staycation caused us to drift in thought even when we were apart,
Real love, our love, had the complete flow to touch, reach, saturate and deeply penetrate our heart.

One we stayed until an unexpected end,
Memories of meaningful moments together with my lover and my friend.

Author: Sherry E. (Jones) Bobbitt
Song Choices: *Baby I'm for Real* by The Originals
Always and Forever by Heatwave

CHAPTER 13: THE PRAYER TO ALWAYS CHERISH THE LITTLE THINGS

This prayer was so deeply special to me because James would often say that he could write a book about "cherishing the little things."

I have never been a picky person. I wasn't the child who complained or fussed about what I couldn't/didn't get. My Pop would say, "Tutter will make the best of or find use for whatever you give her." Ms. Classy (my momma) would say, "If Sherry doesn't care for what she is given, she will make it over, make her own creation and will cherish it." James would say,

> I have never met anybody who gets emotional over small things…things that most people, including myself, wouldn't get moved much about." Sugar Britches, your sexy, creative, passionate and silly little girl ways all speak to my soul like you are the water that I thirst like a husband should for his wife. Though it scares me sometimes, I can NOT live without you. I just can't and there are some people who can see that.

As this prayer stirred up in my spirit, I found myself lying in bed with my pillows soaked from my tears. I was supposed to be taking a nap before going to work, but for some strange reason I was desiring to go into the other bedroom. I was scanning the room when my eyes fell upon the paintings of the white tiger and tigress. At that moment I just fell apart, I couldn't hold back the tears. My mind went to one of those little things that I cherished because James bought the paintings for me.

I love shopping at thrift stores, Goodwill and vintage stores. This is one of my favorite things to do by myself or occasionally with somebody. One Saturday morning I wanted to go to the Goodwill just to see what would catch my eye, make me take a long look or cause me to say, "Oh my." Well, James dropped me off and went to get paid for some electrical worked that he had done. I had some money, but I was going to spend some of his/our money. In "our world" what was mine was his and what was his was mine. When he returned, he came in and told me that he was given a check. To this point, nothing had attracted my attention. He went and found a comfortable chair to sit in while I walked around. He said, "As he was watching me in my joy that he couldn't help but feel my joy from across the room as if something shifted in his spirit."

I walked upon the paintings of the white tiger and tigress. I gasped; such an electrifying shower of passion saturated that place where only James could reach. I saw us!! I saw us in the paintings and that feeling took me to our secret place! I knew exactly where I would hang them! When I came to myself, my hands were on my chest, and I had to have them…I just had to have them. However, when I saw the price, I felt that it was a bit much, but I still wanted them. I just hoped and prayed that they would still be there on Monday morning. I found a few other things, got in line and never said anything to James about the paintings. I had no idea that he saw me and my reaction toward the paintings. I just assumed that he was playing games on his phone. Oftentimes, after finishing my shopping, I would sit in the chair next to him and we would sit a spell. This day was no exception. When I walked over to where he was, I sat down and, as usual, he said he finished his game and asked me did I see anything that I really wanted. I simply replied, "I always see something that I really want. Let's get out of here."

We left, went home and I made some chili while he ran an errand. I couldn't help but think about the paintings. My mind shifted to some other things, and I thought that I was going to watch a movie but dosed off to sleep. The next thing I knew, James was sitting on the side of the bed with one of our favorite chili pies. He said, "Sit up Sugar Britches. Let me wash your face and hands so we can eat." James blessed the food and we watched a movie and fed each other. After we finished eating, he said, "If I had my way, if my money was long enough, I would take you on a trip to every state where they have the best thrift stores, vintage and antique stores. I love you Mrs. Sherry Evonne Jones Bobbitt, my one and only Sugar Britches." I just smiled and then he said, "Take the plate in the kitchen please." I got up with the plate in my hand, walked into the living room and there were the paintings. I could hardly believe what I was seeing – I was totally caught by surprise. I said nothing, grabbed my cell phone, downloaded the song "Candy" by Big Maybelle. He walked into the living room and asked, "May I have this dance my sweet lady?" Well, we didn't make it to our love den until hours later. With all that had taken place, let's just say it was so special until we just slept in the living room.

This chapter has certainly taken me to a place that I will never experience again. Why? There will never be another Mr. James Lynn Bobbitt in my life. I had to download this song as I am finishing up this chapter.

Though my eyes are full of tears, there is a warm feeling in my heart, and I must say the memories still make me blush. Of course, he prayed before we went to sleep but before he did, he shared a very "deep place in his heart" with me. Some of the things that he expressed that night were:

- ♥ He told me that I had no idea the amount of time that he spends "THANKING GOD" for all that he has done through me to give him a "type of love that seems so unreal at times"
- ♥ it causes him to easily lose track of time and come back to himself with a smile on the inside that words could never have enough meaning to explain his feelings
- ♥ how this love also scared him at times because he knew firsthand absolutely how it felt to feel like he had lost me, how I would never understand that type of fear in his heart, especially being that it was his own fault regardless of the influence of the outside interference preying on his weakness
- ♥ With tears he shared how it was beyond even 'thought' what it felt like to see me when he was released from jail, how he knew that I would make sure to have a look to make him feel

"instantly foolish" and at the same time to say one of his favorite phrases: "TO GOD BE THE GLORY." (If you really knew James Bobbitt, you know that was what he would say. Some have even imitated him and, as you are reflecting on him saying that, prayerfully it will bring joy to your heart.

- He shared with me that he could never live without me and "GOD KNOWS IT", how he wouldn't be able to stand to see me smiling with another man and especially seeing a man kissing me. He said, "Hell I would just snap, I wouldn't be the same anymore. No, not in a crazy way but I know that I would never be satisfied with another woman. See you have both fu......... up my head and heart at the same time and if I did get with somebody it would only be just for sex and I would grow cold because I would be wanting you and hurting still because I couldn't have you anymore. I know, before you say anything that you would feel the same way, but I am not 'the writer in our little family' it's you. I am here with you for all of this 'love and joy' that I have prayed for even if I have moments where I don't seem to appreciate you because regardless to what anybody has to say, our life is a book that will be a wonderful blessing to people everywhere and I mean that from the deepest part of my soul.

Well, I just smiled with tears the entire time that he was talking, I didn't make one comment. Somehow it felt like I was inside of James, as he was sharing his heart with me. It was his moment, his exhaling experience, his releasing his heart to flow into my heart to enlarge the place in OUR heart. As I kept listening, my breath was being taken away to a level of love that I knew we had never been before. Wow! It was such an amazing feeling. (I briefly experienced the same feeling while on my laptop with this chapter.) We kissed and our love tasted different and was extremely appetizing for the both of us. Intimacy broke through in such a way as if the flood gates could no longer hold back the forces from the unexpected turbulence in our sea of love. Once the panting from our hearts lowered their voices from between our ears, I could feel his spirit shifting and I silently prayed for God to bless his heart because he was in a place to pray.

The prayer that he prayed for me was,

> LORD!! LORD, I THANK YOU IN THE PRECIOUS WONDERFUL MIGHTY LOVING NAME OF JESUS!! I just want to "THANK YOU" for blessing me with my wife, my friend, my lover, the love of my life, my girlfriend who I fell in love with. Please let her love and passion for cherishing the little things never go away!!! I, even on my day to transition from this life, I want to see and feel these moments because they mean so much to us. It does my heart good to know that such little things can bring on such a blushing smile with a bit of shyness. PLEASE!! bless the both of us to always cherish the little things like they are all fine rare crystals to be placed in a special glass case for only our eyes to see and others if we desire to share. I ask all of these things IN THE PRECIOUS NAME OF JESUS CHRIST!!!! AMEN!!! AMEN!!! AMEN!!!

I said "AMEN" too, then we kissed.

One might say that the song that he sung after he prayed is inappropriate, but it was perfect to me. He sang *Fortunate* by Maxwell. If you have never heard this song before, please listen to it.

As, I am coming to a close of this chapter, I recall one other thing to share about the little things cherished.

One weekend James's cousin Gary and a lady friend came to Nashville. Unexpectedly I had guests for the weekend although I had other plans. Little did I know that it was going to be their last weekend together staying up all night long talking. The weekend turned out wonderful, I cooked the entire time, no meals out. When the time arrived for them to leave, Gary's lady friend finally got a return call from some friends. Gary took her to spend time with them, so he and James decided to go to a sports bar to watch a game. I thought that James was gone to meet Gary but instead he went to H. G. Hills to get me some peach cobbler, vanilla bean ice cream and a lily. I was washing dishes when there was a knock at the door. I could hear his truck so I opened the door. There was my "Little Love Package" in the doorway. He was sitting in his truck and said, "Sugar Britches, thank you baby!! This entire weekend has been, as you say, 'Groovie' and I mean groovie baby! I will be back after the game. Hey, save some ice cream so I can………" and he blew me a kiss. What truly touches the heart, reaches the heart and dwells all through the heart – at least for Mr. & Mrs. James Lynn Bobbitt.

Once again, our passion was displayed and we didn't realize it. Before I could go inside, our neighbor Shondra said , "Ya'll are so damn cute. I'm jealous but my love is coming because looking at you two gives me hope." I replied, "I am truly blessed and I know it!!!!"

I went inside, put my peach cobbler in the oven to warm up, put some in a bowl, placed some ice cream on top, found me a Lifetime movie and enjoyed myself, by myself. While I was enjoying my little love package, my phone rang. It was James. I said, "Hello handsome." He said nothing, but *Lady* by The Whispers was playing and I listened. When the song was over, he said, "I love you lady" and I said, "I love you man. It's all about us" and I hung up.

Little sweet sentiments of love to cherish.

THE PRAYERS THAT HE PRAYED FOR ME

~POEM~

With care and affection "little things" are to be cherished, handle with a loving touch,
After all it's the little unexpected things that mean so much.

To cherish is to hold, to cultivate, to protect, to lovingly care for,
The more that one cherishes, love only thirsts for wanting love more and more.

Such beautiful memories birth from gestures so small,
Love is always awaiting and ready, never needing to receive a call.

Cherished trinkets placed in a special box or displayed for others to see,
Embracing every feeling while blushing with tears because what we have means so much to me.

Many times words were unspoken, tangibility out of reach and eyes could not meet,
Left alone with the most beautiful intimate thoughts while my heart dances in the rain with bare feet.

The afterthoughts of what has been cherished will bring joy in times of need,
Prayers showered over every gift, each time sown like a seed.

To have your heart cherished takes the souls on a passionate intimate flight,
Cherishing the little things truly floods the heart with shades of love that fills the sky and sparkle in the night.

To share feelings in such a special way that stains the heart with the beautiful colors of love and passion that runs extremely deep,
The connection of cherishing moves in special ways, even when the two are embraced as they sleep

Author: Sherry E. (Jones) Bobbitt
My Song Choices: *Oh Honey* by Delegation
I *Wanna Be Closer* by Switch

CHAPTER 14: THE WEDDING ANNIVERSARY PRAYERS

The wedding anniversary prayers were very special. James would wake me up at 12:00 a.m., if I was asleep, to tell me, "Happy Wedding Anniversary Sugar Britches!" I would say, "Happy wedding anniversary Big Daddy!" We observed wedding anniversaries, birthdays, and other special occasions as national holidays for us. Of course, you know prayer was next. Before any type of celebrating, we had to pray. It was just that way and I loved it.

In this chapter I will share his first and last wedding anniversary prayers. I was expecting the first prayer, but I did not know that the reason he was so emotional during our last wedding anniversary celebration was our last.

I will have to brace myself for the last one. I just assumed that he was just overwhelmed because of everything that had taken place that weekend. I wonder if he knew that it was the last time—especially with me hearing him crying in his prayers about never wanting to leave me.

The First Prayer:

> FATHER! FATHER! I just want to THANK YOU for this first year as husband and wife...as Mr. and Mrs. James Lynn Bobbitt. We are so happy and full of joy on our special holiday! This diamond in the rough has loved me, dealt with me, been patient with me and so passionate toward me until it brings chills and I never want this feeling to go away, even in our old age. LORD, we are asking and believing YOU for 50 years of marriage, a golden wedding anniversary. Let this day be full of unexpected surprises. Please give us traveling mercies as

we hit the highway to celebrate this wonderful occasion. LORD! We will begin each wedding anniversary with prayer and thanksgiving! To God be the GLORY for all that YOU have done and all that YOU shall do. We, Mr. and Mrs. James Lynn Bobbitt pray this prayer by faith in JESUS name. AMEN! AMEN! AMEN!

The Second Prayer:

This prayer, the last wedding anniversary prayer, struck me differently. I can't ever say that I felt like it was the last prayer, but I can say, with certainty, that it was deep and very emotional, and I just couldn't shake it. We had a wonderful weekend, but it stayed on my mind. It was the first time that I wanted to ask him why he prayed like that. He cried so hard while holding me tightly as if I may be going away. He seemed to be okay after a while but continued to say how much he loved me, how he regretted everything bad that happened in our marriage relationship because it was always, always his fault. I told him that I made some mistakes over the years, but he insisted that they were like accidentally stepping on somebody's toes, even though it hurt.

Well, I was hoping that his mood would shift to being a little more cheerful because our godfathers were on their way to celebrate our anniversary weekend with us. Finally, Uncle Bill and Uncle Mike were in Nashville. We all chilled a bit and then had dinner. They grilled and brought everything with them. They put me out of my kitchen and served us. We pigged out, played games, listened to music, and enjoyed the evening. The next day we went to brunch, shoe shopping, and out for ice cream. James and I split a cherry while kissing (just nasty but that was us). Uncle Mike took a picture of us. We rode through the city, shopped some more, then back home for showers, naps, rest and later out to dinner. During our time alone, I held James in my arms. He seemed to be in a place where he just needed me that way once again. We fell asleep that way until Uncle Bill woke us up for dinner. We all took a nap. Dinner was very cozy. We held hands most of the night, even from time to time while eating. After dinner, we went downtown for a while. After arriving back at home, we had a happy wedding anniversary toast, more games, music, and plenty of laughter. James made a special toast that had all of us in tears and there I was, again, not thinking that it was the last time, but I couldn't help but be concerned about how overwhelmed he was. Uncle Bill and Uncle Mike retired for the evening and James and I went to sit in the car listening to some *Quiet Storm* which was part of what we did. It was now after midnight, so we went inside because we were going to church. The four of us went to Olivet Missionary Baptist Church, where our dear friend Michael L. Cousin, Sr. is the pastor. After church we came home, ate leftovers and a few hours later the godfathers left.

We certainly enjoyed that very special celebration full of many surprises from the godfathers and each other. We had taken off work that Monday, and also called out Tuesday because we were totally caught up in a segment of *Can't Get Enough of Your Love Baby.*

At midnight James prayed:

> LORD, please make this an extremely wonderful wedding anniversary. Let the memories made from it be cherished in my wife's heart for years to come. Let us be able to love on each other like never before. Let it be like our first time with a combination like it's our last time. We do THANK YOU. I especially THANK YOU for another year, another blessed year to have and to hold each other. Let nothing keep this love from dying LORD. YOU know my heart and you know that I can't get the words out like I want to, but please let her feel the love—feel the need and understand why I'm feeling this way. Keep my wife safe as YOU always have. I am depending on YOU, LORD.

He broke down crying, but continued:

> I am depending on YOU with all my heart. She has been my rock. She stayed with me when others would

have left me. She didn't understand why but trusted YOU enough to get me to this place and, for that, I thank you BOTH. Yes LORD!! YES LORD!! YES LORD!! To YOU be ALLLLLLLLL the honor, praise, and glory!!! Nobody but YOU, LORD, could touch her heart to give me a chance to get it right. I fell a few times and LORD she never tripped. BLESS MY WIFE. She has gifts and YOUR WORD says that her gifts will make room for her. Let them make room for her Lord!! Don't let her leave here without them making room for her!! I'm THANKFUL! I am THANKFUL to have her hand in marriage, her love but most of all her patience. If I had my way, so many things would be done sooner, but I realize that everything is in your time. Help me to stay in my lane and let YOU do this YOUR WAY!!! THANK YOU for letting me see, letting me have a glimpse of those things to come. She will touch lives with our story, her poems, the other books that she has started.

This wedding anniversary I lift up to you Lord…asking for SPECIAL BLESSINGS. YOUR WORD SAYS when a man finds a wife, he finds a good thing and has favor with YOU. THANK YOU! THANK YOU! THANK YOU for my good thing! My Sugar Britches! My girlfriend! My buddy! My lover! My confidant! My teacher! My pastor! My wife! My wife! My only wife! LORD PLEASE! LORD, PLEASE hear my prayer!! In JESUS wonderful name!! AMEN! AMEN! AMEN! AMEN!

He began to worship God. He went in and I joined him. We had never gone in like that before. It was different – on a much deeper level. We ended up on the floor together prostrated before the Lord. Afterwards, we got up, went to bed, held each other tight, fell asleep, waking up in the same position.

I had no idea, NO idea it was our last wedding anniversary prayer together. I took it as our love moving to a new level—not preparing for a departure! That was far from my thoughts. I knew that something heavy was on his heart but leaving me did NOT enter into my spirit. I wondered a few times if I was leaving because of my health.

The Last Wedding Anniversary Prayer!

I must admit that my heart is still broken. Many people say that after all of this time, I should not still feel this way; but I say, "If you weren't married to James Bobbitt, how can you understand where I am and how I am feeling?" Huge pieces of the puzzle in my life are missing forever and I won't get them back.

My Tutter, Elder Felecia Moore, told me that my heart had many chambers and there is a chamber in my heart that's only meant for James Bobbitt…no one else, but don't shut my whole heart.

One of James' dear brother/friend, Pastor Michael Cousin, told me that he knew James well enough to know that my present state of mind would sadden James and he wouldn't want me crying the way that I do. James' sister/friend, Minister Freda Cousin, tells me all of the time, "My Tutta, I just keep you in prayer because I know, and I don't know He adored you and so many married women don't know what it is like to be adored by their husband. What a blessing, what a blessing!

~POEM~

Embedded in a special chamber of my heart are the wedding anniversary prayers that James prayed each year,
Time and absence can never move that which was and still is to me so dear.

Tears and kisses were always in their place after every AMEN we said together hand in hand,
Blessed to embrace another year with me being his woman and him being my man.

Looking at our wedding pictures was always a part of the day,
Reflecting and remembering when we couldn't wait to hear the phrase husband and wife, nearly not paying much attention to the other things that Rev. Martin had to say.

There were many times we took trips, celebrated with others but found the best times were spent home alone,
Deeply being into each other, not wanting to be disturbed and turning off the telephone.

Celebrating was important to make wonderful memories to cling to,
Every year we had our own private ceremony standing face to face saying, "I Do."

The many years of prayers, celebrations, and memories flooded my soul when I found myself, for the first time, on that special day all alone,
Another crushing in my heart because no matter how sweet the memories were, he was gone.

Over the years many people have said, "He is still with you." That may be so but it's not the same,
The day he left my title changed from Mrs. To Ms., which is devastating to me and changing the flow of my name.

I am left to look at his picture wishing a wish that can't come true,
Dealing with the shift in my life, unable to stand face to face has turned my world misty blue.

Author: Sherry E. (Jones) Bobbitt
My Song Choices: *Still Standing Tall* by The Williams Brothers
Anniversary by Tony Tone Toni

CHAPTER 15: THE PRAYER FOR THE RIGHT SISTAS IN MY LIFE

This was an area in my life that James was serious about and very much concerned with. There were certain women that he felt would cause me harm in many ways. He got to this place after confiding in one who he thought was a sista to me. I was going through something, and he felt that if he shared with her, she could help him help me. He was looking for a woman's view on what I was dealing with. Well, as it turned out, she waited until there was an opportunity for me to advance and brought up my weak moment, exposed me and she only had the ammunition to do so because James confided in her. She acted as if she was a real sista.

This made James extremely furious. He could not believe that she would do such a thing—especially with her being a First Lady and a minister. He went off on her.

To sum up his feelings concerning me and women being close to me, I do believe that Pastor Sondrea Tolbert said it best at his homegoing celebration. She said, "She felt privileged to be one of the other women in his life. He showed her, through his brotherly love for her, just how much he trusted her with me and that there weren't many women that he trusted as my sista."

One may find this strange, but I found it beautiful and caring. He had his own list. That was just how he was, and he didn't make his list any secret. He would check anybody in my circle down to the wire, letting me know who he was uncomfortable with and told some to their face how he felt.

The sistas that he said were God SENT, he prayed for them, loved them and did his part to protect them. They all knew that they were his girls. Pastor Tolbert would say, "She was the other woman." She bought the last full meal that he tried to eat. She fed him. When she got to the door to leave, she turned, blew a kiss at him and stuck her tongue out at me. It was the last time that the three of us were together. Two days later, he was gone. She and my other sistas drove to Trenton, TN to be with me on the day of his homegoing. She was the first one that I saw. She was there when I got there, and she sat next to me holding my hand. The others were there holding my hand also.

The other sistas that he felt fine about being in my circle are: Pastor Sherry Goodlow-Allen, Lady/Minister Freda Cousin, Elder Felecia Moore, Minister Brenda Hewlett, Pastor Marilyn McClain, Pastor Brenda Young, Pastor Ollie Cheatum, Evangelist Annice Springer, Lady Betty Smith, Sister Nancy Roberson, Evangelist LaVelle Walker, Evangelist Betty Lynch, Evangelist Watkins, Rev. Versie Easter, Rev. Wilma Walden-Pearson, Evangelist Evonne Scruggs, Rev. Donita Flippin, Minister Tonya Johnson-Cantrell, Evangelist Sondra Cooks, Oreva Childs, Gail Carter, Marilyn Avinger and Angela Burrows (Deceased). Ms. Verbenna Harrison bka BeBe was a special mother figure and big sister rolled into one loving person. James trusted her with our lives. He had a personal relationship with all of them and loved them like sistas and they all knew it. They all have their personal stories about their relationship with James. He did whatever he could for them all. I remember the last time he saw Freda Cousin, my Tutta. It was her birthday. She was shocked to see him because he had only been out of the hospital for a couple of days, but he insisted. As it turned out, it was his last time celebrating her birthday with her. He passed away two weeks later. She posts a picture of them hugging on Facebook often.

After I was betrayed, he felt the need to pray for me and the women who were/are to enter into my life up close. His prayer:

> FATHER! FATHER! Please hear this prayer. I have made a terrible mistake thinking that all women in leadership roles in church were trustworthy. I have hurt my wife, not on purpose, in my effort to help. I have hurt her by sharing her pain with someone who I thought that loved her as a sister. I don't know much about

discernment, knowing when and when not to trust those who claim to have an anointing. I am asking in the mighty name of JESUS CHRIST for the way or ways to know who should and should not be around my wife. Maybe I am not using the right words in this prayer but LORD, YOU know my heart and how my heart felt when I was reaching out for help that plotted to hurt. I didn't do what I wanted because my wife asked me not to but LORD, as I have the hands of my wife/YOUR DAUGHTER, please bless her, protect her and keep her safe from women wo will not understand her walk with YOU. I can't be with my wife on every occasion where she speaks because I know some things are just for women only. So, I need other women. As my wife says, "There are sisters and there are sistas. Well, I really need for you to surround her with sistas who have her best interest at heart, women who will help and not hurt. She is blessed by YOU to be who she is, and I need other women to see that as well. Let her even know when she should cut women off who really don't mean her any good.

As YOU continue to let her DOWN IN THE DEEP TREASURES Of YOUR LOVE and UNDERSTANDING, give her that thing that she needs when to trust and when not to trust, when to accept invitations and when not to, when to eat or drink and when not to because I am finding out that people do some crazy things that claim to FOLLOW YOU. All I know is I don't want this to happen to my wife again. I need to know what to do, what to say, what to look for, what to feel, what to be aware of and, most of all, how to pray concerning women in my wife's midst. This is so important to me LORD because she needs to be free to go and do what YOU have CALLED her to do. As I have my hands on her, please give her what she needs because I am limited and, if for some strange reason that this happens again, give us wisdom on how to deal with it. I am asking this in THE POWERFUL, WONDERFUL NAME OF JESUS CHRIST, OUR SAVIOR and REDEEMER. I pray this prayer by faith! AMEN! AMEN! AMEN!

As these sistas entered my life James was constantly in prayer concerning them. One day he looked at me and said, "You've got to know who is in your life for a season, a reason or a lifetime. Honey, this I can't know for you. You will have to know so you can let me know."

Strange as it was, but yet so true, there was great reasons for the way that he felt. The other sista that said just about the same as Pastor Tolbert is Minister Brenda Hewlett that he depended on as well. She would say, "Bobbitt don't play when it comes to his wife, and he will let you know just that." When I was about to be ordained, he called Brenda (Hewlett) Day and asked her to pick up our moms and bring them to Nashville with her and she did gladly and took them both back to their homes.

I must also include two special daughters: Connie Cousin (Niecy Poo), one of James's favorite songbirds and Tameka (Childs) Gibson. These women had their own unique relationship with James. Part of the uniqueness of Tameka's relationship with him was the fact that they always called each other "loser". For them this was a term of endearment that only they could use.

I could go on with the stories about James and my sistas and our daughters.

I must also mention the brothers/men that he trusted. We have a special son who came into our lives shortly after we moved to Nashville in the late 1990's. Marlin Glen shared a lot of our firsts in life and in ministry. He was a strong participant and supporter of all that we did.

Others were/are: the late Rev. Norman Carver (my spiritual big brother), the late LeRoy Spindle (my spiritual father), Elder Grady L. Cooks, Jr., Pastor Michael Cousin, Sr. (my Bubba), Johnny Ray Thomas (his cousin/brother), Rev. Michael Flippin, Pastor Mario Johnson (our spiritual son), Lamont Cousin (Jureeka) and Michael Cousin, Jr., bka Junebug (our babies).

Deacon Robert Boseman was a special friend with whom James had a deep bond. When they met, there was an instant connection between them. Their relationship was closer than some biological brothers. In the wee hours of the morning that Robert passed away, I dreamed that he and James were having devotion together. It wasn't until later in the day that I learned that Robert had passed. At his funeral, I leaned over and whispered in his ear, "Just because you and James are together again, don't be starting no trouble and get put out." Robert's wife, Pat, knew how close they were so when I shared with her what I said, even in her grief, it made her laugh and we hugged. Another special friend, who was more like a little brother, was Vincent Burrows. They took many road trips together. Vincent is now deceased also.

James's friends/brothers had, and have, stories about his list. Yes, James had a list. Pastor Cousin officiated James' Celebration of Life service and he mentioned the list and said, "He was glad that he wasn't on 'the list'.

Elder Cooks was my mentor as I was preparing to be ordained. Once I called James as his girlfriend. James had the call on speaker because he was driving. I asked, "Where is your wife?" James said, "She's at work, what up with you pretty lady?" I said, "I need to see you, baby I miss you." James said, "I miss you too; let's meet at our spot."

Elder Cooks was with James and very upset with him. He told James, "Now I love you and your lovely wife both and I didn't like that. You need to take me home." Trying not to laugh, James said, "Don't trip with me. I really got to see her. We're just going to eat lunch; I want you there to meet her. I believe that you will like her. Elder Cooks was hot. He told James, "I don't feel good about this at all." Meanwhile, I was on my way to meet them. When I arrived, I put on sunglasses and a scarf. I walked in, went right up to the table where they were sitting and gave James a long kiss then turned around and said, "What's up Grady Cooks, Jr.?" His face was classic. He was totally shocked. He said, "You two play too much. I'm sitting here upset with my boy here and ready to check this situation once you got here and it's you." I said, "How are you going to be mad at him because he wanted to see his girlfriend? You better be glad I didn't want to meet at a hotel, now what?" He was done with me. We laugh about that now.

Michael Cousin has had to ask James to put his knife away on a few occasions. James was a Peter but also one that would be there for you when nobody else would be. Michael is the husband of my Tutta, Freda Cousin. We spent a lot of time with these two, a part of the family and I still am.

James always called Rev. Michael Flippin Bishop Flip. It didn't matter where James saw him, he would yell across the store, parking lot or wherever he saw him. He had to get a hug and shake hands with Rev. Flippin. Rev. Carver was also my mentor/loving big brother/advisor. Elder Spindle was our spiritual father. I miss all of the conversations that he had with James and me. He was there to be my "mother bird" as he would say when I accepted my calling. A few days later before he passed away, he came by the church. He had been out of town and not expected to be there, but he came in just after the evening program ended. I was in the kitchen cleaning. He came in yelling, "Where is my baby bird?! Where is my baby bird?!" James told him that I was in the kitchen, so he came in there. With tears rolling down his cheeks he said, "Flap your wings baby bird as I flap mine." As we stood face to face crying and flapping our wings, he said, "You listen to me, and you listen good. It's time for me to put you out of the nest. It's time for you to fly, to soar without me. I will be watching over you, but you must fly without me because you won't need me anymore." That upset me and I said, "I will always need you. Please don't say that." His reply was, "I came to tell you that I've done all that I could, and birds don't stay in the nest forever. So fly away little bird. Soar! There is so much for you to do, this old robin red breast's wings are growing weak." He hugged me very tight and walked away. I didn't know what to think. He went and hugged James and left. A few days later he passed away.

James and Ray were like brothers, but they were first cousins. They talked just about every day. In the last months of James' life, they would talk sometimes three times a day. There were many times when the three of us would talk, he would tell Ray to talk to me while he got himself together and then tell me and Ray that time was up, we have talked too long. Ray and I laugh about that when we talk. Ray got to know James, the James that I knew and love on a deeper level, a spiritual level that Ray didn't know about. With that, he got to know me as well through their relationship. James shared a lot with Ray concerning our marriage relationship. Ray was a huge support to James when he was extremely sick. He made sure that he talked to James every day which meant a lot to James and to me. He has also been one of my biggest encouragers to write this book—one of many that he knew James wanted me to write. Ray always reminds me of the conversations that James would have with him concerning my gift of writing.

What can I say about Mario? He just stepped in and became a son. He has been there through some of most worst meltdown moments after losing James. He would stay at the hospital in the wee hour of the morning. One day he stayed all evening until midnight, having to drive back to base and be on the ship by 8:00 a.m. He is in the United States Navy. He made it by a few minutes. That was the last day he spent with James in the hospital.

James rested well with it in his heart that I had sons to love me. He trusted that Mario, Lamont, Junebug and Marlin would be those sons and they have.

James had a very wonderful relationship with Michael and Freda Cousin's sons, and they were very much okay with sharing all of their babies with us.

Marlin was there for both of our times in the hospital. He was there when things didn't look good for me and a support to James as he was dealing with me being so sick for so long. One special Christmas, I was very sick in the hospital. I was feeling down. I had been in the hospital since the second Tuesday in September. I had gotten upset, and the nurse gave me something so I could calm down and get some rest. When I woke up, my room looked like a Christmas village. James had come in while I was sleep and set things up. It was so beautiful. As I was crying at how special James was making things, in walks Marlin and his girlfriend singing.

Marlin walked over to the bed and said, "Hey mama." He kissed me and they sat down. James said, "Let's have a toast." Because I was in the hospital, we didn't have champagne. Instead, we had white sparkling grape juice. James said, "We are toasting to me still being with him." Afterwards, we sung R&B Christmas carols with the radio. We enjoyed our time together. Before we knew, it was after 2:00 a.m.—officially Christmas Day. Marlin and his girlfriend left, and my Big Daddy walked over to me and said, with tears rolling down his face, "Sugar Britches, I don't want you to be upset because you weren't able to buy me Christmas gifts this year. I have the gift that money could never buy. God has blessed me to still be able to look at, have and hold, my beautiful wife." Then he told me to move over and get some of this 2005 Christmas loving that you've never had before. As you can figure, if you knew the Bobbitts, what took place from there. A Christmas that I will always remember and cherish. I thank God that we were able to make some of the worst times the most happiest and rememberable times. Christmas in the hospital with my Big Daddy.

James mentored and trained deacons and deaconess, but one special bond that he had was with Deacon Gary Simpson. I so wanted Deacon Simpson to share his memories of James in this book, but God saw fit to take him home. Gary and James met through Ambassadors for Christ Ministries where Rev. Michael and Rev. Donita Flippin are Co-Pastors. Gary was considering becoming a Deacon in their ministry and James just connected to Gary right away. Gary always acknowledged James for being the support that he needed during his Deacon training and James was so proud of his little brother becoming a Deacon. James loved being a Deacon and always shared the importance of the call to such a status. I dreamed that James and Gary were having devotion in a church setting. They were both looking well and healthy. Hours later, I saw where Gary passed away. Their relationship blossomed a relationship with Gary's beautiful wife, Shelia and me. We are sistas for life. Love me some Shug!

I know that James prayed concerning these gentlemen whether they were brothers or sons in my life and those to come after him. He told me so.

Particularly concerning the sons, he knew how disappointed I was not to have my dream to give birth to five kings who rightfully were born with the Bobbitt name.

I have been blessed with other sons since James has been gone. They all speak well of James as if they knew him and they keep me covered in prayer and encouraged just like their other brothers. Apostle Sean Miles, Prophet Dwayne Tyler, Bishop Deremus Jones and Junior Boykin all call me "Momma Bobbitt." All of my sons' wives and children have love for me as well. LORD know that I need them all!!

Again, one may find it strange for him to pray in this manner, but he did, and I would not change one thing about his method of praying. He knew there were so many things that were beyond his control, and he deeply depended on God for those things.

I truly THANK God for these wonderful sistas, brothers, sons and daughters, that I didn't mention, for being in the life and times of James and Sherry Bobbitt. The daughters are a book that I hope to write some day!

~POEM~

One day my love prayed for true sistas to enter into my life,
He asked this of God because he couldn't always be there for his wife.

A prayer of protection from things seen and unseen,
He deeply felt the need after trusting one that turned out to be mean.

He also prayed a special prayer concerning the brothers in my life too,
Trusting them to only do the things that God had assigned them to do.

When James realized that it was going to take a village of love and care,
He began to fleece after God because alone it was too much for him to bare.

What unique stories they all have to tell about the James Bobbitt that they knew,
He often referred to them at times, 'The Prayed About Crew'.

I had this Incredible man to love, who took the time to pray concerning those who were to be close to me,
Above all trusting God to be with me then and now that he can no longer be.

Author: Sherry E. (Jones) Bobbitt
My Song Choices: *That's What Friends Are For* by Dionne Warwick
I Need You to Survive by Hezekiah Walker
and The Love Fellowship Choir

CHAPTER 16: THE PRAYER TO MOVE ON AND LIVE LIFE

I must say that this was not a prayer that I wanted to hear or accept. I actually refused to pray with him. He asked me several times and we had conversations about what we had promised each other. He even brought up the fact that just as I wasn't feeling this type of prayer, neither was he when I was very sick. Point being taken, I let him talk and pray. This wasn't a conversation that I wanted to have with him because his words were as if he was throwing me away, even though that wasn't the case.

I sat on the bed, looking at him as he spoke about how blessed he was to have my hand in marriage. He spoke of how he regretted, in some ways, loving me so deeply and hard because it was going to make my journey without him so much harder to combat. He also spoke of how he was still praying for more time with me, how time wasn't ours to control, how life is so important, how he regretted wasting time being foolish, nearly loosing what we had as husband and wife. He regretted allowing outside interference to cause us to lose some precious time together. He cried saying, "If he could turn back the hands of time, there was so many things that wouldn't have happened, and they would all be replaced with only loving me more" and then he went into prayer. He prayed:

> FATHER! FATHER! I really need YOU to move in my wife's life. I can't say exactly when, but she will definitely need YOU. She is only praying with me because I asked her to. The truth is I am not feeling it but we both need YOU for all of the things to come. Cancer is not an issue for me; leaving My Sugar Britches is the issue. It is the issue LORD. If for whatever YOUR REASONS our marriage will come to an end, please, please KEEP YOUR ARMS AROUND MY WIFE. I

have asked things of her that many will say, 'James didn't say that; James wouldn't say that, she's lying.' So, I am asking YOU, with her present, to protect her heart so when the time does come, she will do the things that I have asked of her when she is ready in her heart to do them and give her the strength and courage to do all that I have asked of her when my time comes. Let her do things as we have talked about and let the people, including family, say what they want. I know, as crazy as it may seem to some people, from Maze being played, to having married couples kiss and my baby eulogizing me, it's what I want. Just as wreaths with hats and lilies, love songs playing, having married couples kiss, her sistas and nieces reading her love poems, are some of her requests for her celebration of life.

My mind and heart is all over the place praying this prayer because I am not trying to make her cry. I am not trying to make us cry because we asked you for a certain time for this but, at the moment, I just can't be sure. My God! My God! Have mercy on ME!! AMEN! AMEN! AMEN!

All we could do was cry; I only had my faith and was hoping that James would just get well. Even though through frustration of being helpless I would say, "Heal Him or Take Him." There were times that I felt so very helpless, watching him hurting, losing weight, feeling less of a man because he had to depend on me for everything. I made absolutely sure that he totally understood that I didn't mind anything that I had to do, no matter how many times I had to do it. He would say, "Baby, I know that you don't, but I do." Those words would break my heart. I am in tears as I write because the pain of being so helpless is still with me. Even, after him telling me that there was nothing else for me to do, I kept reaching, through prayer, for something—for what I couldn't find.

When the doctors told us that James had six months to a year to live, I truly felt that there was both time and hope for a miracle. I had no idea, as I have already stressed, that he would go the same day after we were given a timeframe.

I just could not believe what God allowed. I just couldn't and so soon after this prayer to go through with the plans that James wanted. That wasn't going to set well with his mother and others. So many times I wished that he, himself, could have shared this very important plan of his because it definitely wasn't my plan. My dream was shattered into a million pieces, and I was left with a matter that needed to be taken care of quickly.

Losing the love of my life and our baby girl J'Meese were the worst things that ever happened to me. I found myself making plans that I wasn't ready to make, noise all around me, doing what I could to keep and maintain peace all around me all the while knowing that my methods would be misunderstood. Unbeknown to others, in prior years, James and I discussed how things were to be done for both of us when the time came. While Chester Baskerville was showing Kesha, James and me caskets for my mother, James asked him about a casket for himself. Though I found it strange at that moment, James was excited to make this decision, so I didn't have to. He wanted to make it easier for me in the decision-making process and I would have less to do. He also chose the colors and the dress and hat that we wanted me to wear for his funeral service. Additionally, he whispered in my ear, "Don't forget my white carnations and red roses for my spray." Given his unique personality and way of doing things, James requested for music by Frankie Beverly and Maze to be played. I spoke with Pastor Darrick Theus beforehand to inform him so he would be aware. Pastor Theus gave his approval and even commented that James reminded him of Frankie Beverly when he was wearing his white cap. Another detail that James reiterated to me was that he wanted me to eulogize him. But before I started the eulogy, I was to tell married couples to kiss each other as an expression of love for each other and in honor of him and his love for marriage. It was his life, his service, his last request and because of my tremendous love for him, I honored his every request, although I pointed out to him the ridicule I would receive from others. Despite my concerns, he took my hands and said, “Honey do it for me.”

I still can’t bring myself to get his headstone, but I keep in mind that he told me to do it when I got ready. Left with my tears, fears and so many wonderful memories of years with James Lynn Bobbitt.

THE PRAYERS THAT HE PRAYED FOR ME

~POEM~

Deeply wounded living a life that I'd rather not live,
Many times feeling like there's no more love left in me to give.

Tilling, sowing and faithfully cultivating together the ground that we had
Now pulling the plow by myself leaves me lonesome and sad.

Voices speaking God has a better plan for your life,
If only they could see in my heart one that was molded and shaped to be a loving wife.

Move on! Move on! comes from the chants of those who say they care,
With all of the noise, nobody has yet to say where.

Feeling like a poor wind that nobody is aware of,
Searching for the olive branch in the mouth of a dove.

Nights are so long and dark,
My heart no longer flickers or has a spark.

Shoes that can never be filled by another,
Not even having a comforting arm of my mother.

Alone in the room with my thoughts louder than my voice,
My response continues to be "I'm living the life of no other choice."

Until the hand of God moves to fill this empty space,
My heart will continue to have the look of a sad face.

I refuse to pretend that the pain is not there,
With all the encouragement rendered, to me life right now is not fair.

Say what you will and say what you want about my faith and about my belief,
You won't understand what I understand until the tears flow from that place of relief.

So if you're tired of seeing me cry, please turn the other way,
You can't desire more than I do to see a brighter day.

Author: Sherry E. (Jones) Bobbitt
My Song Choice: *Missing You* by Diana Ross

CHAPTER 17: THE LAST PRAYER THAT HE PRAYED FOR ME

Around 7:00 p.m. things were settling down after James got to hospice. The doctors sent him there for pain management; he would only be there for three days. He wanted everybody to leave. He kept saying, "I really appreciate all of the visitors, but I need my quality time with you Sugar Britches. I just need our quality time."

Quality time meant soooooooooooooo much to us. It was often misunderstood by many, but we needed that, and I am so glad that we were able to turn off the noise and get to our quality time. Quality time and personal touches – imagine not getting either.

Once everybody left, he told the nurses to hurry and do all that they had to do because he needed some quality time with his wife. The nurses honored his request.

He asked me to come and sit on the bed; I did. He kept kissing my hands with tears rolling down his cheeks. Naturally I was crying too. Then he said:

> You have been so wonderful throughout this cancer situation. Baby you have been right by my side. The nurses and doctors always compliment me not having any type of body odor and no signs of bedsores. You have taken such good care of me. You didn't put me in a nursing home. You took care of me and Claris (my mom) at the same time, running from room to room. Our home was always clean. You kept me dressed nice, even if it meant changing my clothes many times a day (LOL). You just about wiped the black off of me, kept me well groomed, never got mad when I peed on you, threw up on

> you. Baby I couldn't ask for more. I couldn't ask for more. Honey, you never demeaned me.
>
> When I got to the place where I couldn't make love to you, you just said that we have to find other ways to love on each other and how ever that I could love on you would be perfect. Baby you don't know what that means to a man. I had a friend to tell me, before I got this sick, that you would change but I told him, 'Not my girl' and baby you haven't. You have centered your entire life around me and what I need and for that, I love you more than you will ever know. I thought about my mother not wanting me to marry you; hell, that would have been the biggest mistake of my life. You have been my world. I can't imagine how life would be without you. Hell, yes, I can and it wouldn't be a pretty picture. I know that you are so very tired. I wanted to kick it with my friends and family for my birthday and you made it happen. A few days later I wanted to go to Indianapolis; you took me. It was so sweet of you to pull the car over around the corner from Waller and Martha's and let me drive up in the driveway and you let me pull off when we left to come home. Girl, you have always had my back.
>
> Look at how beautiful that garden is. Go open the blinds all the way. Sit down in the recliner. Get off of your feet, they are so swollen. Let's just look at the garden. Maybe tomorrow we can take a walk. Close your eyes and let me sing to you.

I did as he asked of me and he sung our wedding song, *Always and Forever* by Luther Vandross.

I drifted off to sleep and had a wonderful dream. I dreamed that James, J'Meese and I were in the garden, just the three of us. It was different from the one outside of his room. This had a beautiful sparkling bridge, butterflies, birds and lilies everywhere and we could hear music. Our baby girl looked so pretty. She walked up to me and gave me a pink lily. She then took James by the hand and said, "Hi daddy!" James said, "My baby. I am standing here with both of my best girls." For some reason I sat down, but they went for a walk. James looked so fine to me, it made me very emotional, but I kept my seat. The next thing that I knew, they were on that bridge and, at the same time, they said, "See you later!" I woke up because James was calling my name. He was rather upset and said, "Baby, hurry up and come here. I need to pray, and I got to pray right now."

I got up quickly and stood beside him. He took my hand and began praying:

> Father, Father please, please take care of my wife. She has been through so much in a short period of time. She lost her stepmother, her mother, BeBe, Grandma Brown and so many others in less than nine months. She's gonna need YOU LORD!! Keep YOUR LOVING ARMS around my wife. Hold her heart in YOUR HANDS. Protect her as she continues to honor all of my requests of her. People are going to say all manners of things, especially my folks but let her stay strong. You know what I have asked of her; it will be hard, but I know that she will stand firm. You know what we have talked about, the type of homegoing that I want. Let her have courage to do as planned, just like she and I have talked about each other's homegoing celebrations. This LORD! Cancer has never been my fear; my fear is leaving my wife. I don't want to leave my wife anytime soon but it's YOUR WILL, not my will be done. I love my wife. My soul aches right now! LORD, there is a wonderful journey that she can't see, but please lead and guide my Sugar Britches to and through this journey. Keep everybody that will bring her harm far away from her—even if it means family.

> Help her when she gets to those places of not understanding YOU! Oh LORD! My LORD!! AMEN!!

All of a sudden, he got upset, He wanted me to hug him. He kept saying, "I know that you don't understand but I must say things while I am able to." I said, "Ok honey." He kept looking at me crying – we were crying. He kept saying how much he loved me, and he wished that we got our vision. I said, "Baby, don't upset yourself. We will take this one day at a time and continue to make the best of each day we have left. He said, "I know that you love you some James Lynn Bobbitt. I know that you would make each day count and that I can cherish them in my spirit. Forever mine!! Forever mine!!"

We kissed and kissed. As I was wiping his tears, he said, "Where is my sister? Where is Dovie? We used to be so close. I need to see my sister." I said "Ok." I called Dovie and told her that James was very upset and wanted to see her. She and Jeremy (her son) came back to the hospital. Before they got there James was so irritated the nurse wanted to give him something for pain. He refused because he said that he had more to talk to me about.

Dovie and Jeremy got there quickly. She and James talked. She told him that everything was going to be alright. She and Jeremy sat down in the room with us. James was trying to tell me something. He was having difficulty getting his words together. So, he kept saying, "I love you Sherry." He squeezed my hands and we kissed. I told him that I loved him too, that I always will, nothing will ever change that. He said "Sherry Evonne Jones Bobbitt, thank you for your hand in marriage. Thank you for being my wife. Thank you for your love. I love you Sugar Britches. I love you, Sherry!

I told him that I loved him so much. I asked him not to hurt for me. I said, "When the time comes, though I don't want it, when God says, 'LET'S GO JAMES, you go! He looked at me with that James Bobbitt smile and said, "Sherry, I love you." He took a very deep breath and left me.

My soul felt as if it was ripped out. I told Dovie that he was gone. The nurse came in and told me that he wasn't She checked for his pulse and listened to his heart. My man/my husband was gone.

I lost my only child, our baby girl. I lost my parents, a sister, two brothers, a beautiful stepmother, a wonderful father-in-law, my grandparents (on both sides), aunts, uncles, cousins, dear friends and all of them together doesn't compare to losing James. I don't believe anything will ever hurt me so deeply again. You couldn't have made me believe that it was the last prayer that he would pray for me. No, absolutely not! I thought that we had at least months; prayerfully some more years. I wrapped my mind around one month, one day at a time…not hours.

He kept telling me that there was nothing else for me to do. I had gone beyond the call of duty and how much he loved me for all that I had done. I did not see it coming, even after dreaming about the three of us in the garden. I just chalked everything up as preparing me for weeks or months to come.

Now I have these wonderful memories—especially the wonderful blessings of memories of prayers just for me. I know that I am extremely blessed. I have found that many married couples do not have a prayer life together and that hurts because the majority of our married friends are believers.

~POEM~

I had a man, a boyfriend, a lover, a friend, a husband, a priest of my home and heart who prayed for me,
With a heart that TRUST God to handle all that he didn't know and could not see.

In spite of his ups and downs, he believed in the power of prayer,
For him it wasn't just enough to love; he also knew that there would be things in life, as a husband, that would be too much for him alone to bare.

Seeing him on his knees praying was spiritually sexy without an ounce of lust,
His manhood was never intimated to seek the God that he completely trust.

I always loved when he could sense that I was standing, just watching him pray,
He simply held out his hand, inviting me to join him without interrupting what he had to say.

Prayers in bed were so precious to me too,
Locked in his arms until the morning light loving hearing him say
"THANK YOU LORD and good morning, Boo."

My life feels very empty now that I pray all alone,
So many times I find myself on my knees in tears without a word to say now that he's gone.

Sometimes while praying I can feel James near,
Loving memories of a prayer life with my love; forever in my heart I will hold ever so dear.

Author: Sherry E. (Jones) Bobbitt
My Song Choices: *It's So Hard to Say Goodbye to Yesterday* by G. C. Cameron
I Miss You by Harold Melvin and The Blue Notes

FINAL THOUGHTS

James's and my prayers were, and mine continue to be, that this book was worth your time reading it. I hope there was something, in at least one chapter, that will benefit or enhance your marriage relationship and help you develop a healthy prayer life together as an engaged couple.

Prayer is very important. I feel that always including God is a plus! Life comes with many unexpected twists and turns. Everyone doesn't want to see married couples together. The enemy doesn't want you to have a loving marriage. Consequently, he certainly doesn't want you to include prayer and/or have a healthy prayer life together.

Again, I am in tears because marriage is a beautiful union between two people; the most intimate transparent relationship that you can have with anyone. There is never time to waste on the meaningless things that come to divide and conquer.

Love while there is still life as we know it. Don't compare relationships. Do what works for yours and do it with the attitude "I don't kiss and tell." If you do, do it in order to help a married couple in trouble, but always pray first. Use wisdom. Encourage them to sit down and communicate WITH each other—not AT each other and discover the joys of what's going to work for them.

Marriage is a wonderful place to bask in. I truly miss what I had, but I must utilize what I had to spread a seasoned word of encouragement.

For those who ***really*** know me, you already know how I am coming – simply real, raw and just keeping it 1000. Time is never on our side. We can't see time, we can't hold time, we can't stop time and we don't fully understand the essences of time. We just get to move through and in time. So why waste time?

James's prayer and message for you:

LORD, let everybody who picks up these books that you bless my wife to write, be blessed by our story—especially this book. I won't be around to shake your hand and tell you 'thank you' so I do so in this prayer that my queen is sharing from my heart to your heart. She didn't understand why this book...this book about us had to be written after I was gone. Real simple...the outcome.

I pray that a healthy prayer life is developed or enhanced in your marriage. All I know is we couldn't have our story without God! LORD, let whoever is reading this not wonder why I am praying and talking. I am in great pain, and I must say what's on my mind while I can. Marriage is all about love IN love together which includes God. I really hope and pray that you have this understood and, if not, that you will very soon. I wasted some precious time and was truly blessed to have more time to get it right. LORD, I lift up every married couple that will read this book and ask that they experience love on the next level. In the words of my queen, 'Love taking you to a level that you had no idea that such a place was possible to enter into together; a place that only God can allow married couples to enter into that have deemed themselves worthy to bask in'...just how my Sugar Britches saw it.

BLESS AS ONLY YOU CAN LORD. Protect, lead and guide these marriages in the mighty name of JESUS CHRIST OUR SAVIOR and REDEEMER!! In HIS name I do pray! AMEN! AMEN! AMEN!

Well, I made it. I did it. With tears, I have completed a task...one that my love asked of me. It has been hard, very hard, but I am here. What's next? I can't say.

I am learning how to continue this journey without my husband/my love by my side. A Journey that was chosen for me, one that I call "a journey of no other choice."

On James' last day on this side, we held hands crying, thanked God for our life together and our story for me to write. We thank you, in advance. James wanted you to know how much he appreciated your love and support. I just didn't realize his rush for all that he had to say was because time was up for him. My thoughts were maybe he would be too sick later on – not because he was hours away from leaving me.

Again, THANK YOU! Many have wondered about the prayers that I prayed for my beloved husband James. Before you obtained our book, it was placed in my spirit that you may wonder about the prayers that I prayed for him while you were reading about the ones he prayed for me. Seeds of life have been placed within me once again. Soon to be birthed…the sequel…*The Prayers I Prayed for Him.*

There is one thing that I really miss – God, James and Sherry Bobbitt. I miss the THREE of us!!!

Song Choices: *Gone too Soon* by Michael Jackson
I Wanna Thank You by Frankie Beverly and Maze